SEARCHING FOR AMERICA

SEARCHING FOR AMERICA

VOLUME ONE: THE NEW WORLD

WRITTEN BY ZACHARY HAMBY
EDITED BY RACHEL HAMBY

DEDICATION

For the Puritans and Pilgrims, whose dream of

a city on a hill has become our own

Our fathers' God to Thee,
Author of liberty,
To Thee we sing.
Long may our land be bright,
With freedom's holy light,
Protect us by Thy might,
Great God, Our King.

"My Country 'Tis of Thee"
Samuel Francis Smith

ISBN-10: 0-9827049-6-8
ISBN-13: 978-0-9827049-6-7

Searching for America, Volume One: The New World
Written and Illustrated by Zachary Hamby
Edited by Rachel Hamby
Published by Hamby Publishing in the United States of America

Copyright © 2018 Hamby Publishing

All rights reserved. Portions of this book may be photocopied for classroom use only. No portion of this book may be reproduced in any form or by any electronic or mechanical means, including information storage and retrieval systems, without permission in writing from the publisher, except by a reviewer, who may quote brief passages in review. Special permissions are required for commercial or public performances of these scripts. Contact the author for more information about the fees associated with these types of performances.

TABLE OF CONTENTS

INTRODUCTORY MATERIALS

Searching for America: An Introduction to the Series	7
Using This Book in the Classroom	9
American Dreamers: An Introduction for Students	11

SCRIPT-STORIES: THE NEW WORLD

The Flying Canoe	13
Gluscabi	25
The Explorers of the New World	37
Mayflower: The Voyage of the Pilgrims	49
The Courtship of Miles Standish	61
Captured by Indians	73
The Journey of Olaudah Equiano	89
The Scarlet Letter: Part I	105
The Scarlet Letter: Part II	117
The Scarlet Letter: Part III	131
The Scarlet Letter: Part IV	143

SUPPLEMENTAL MATERIALS

New World Colony-Building Game   157

About the Author   161

SEARCHING FOR AMERICA
AN INTRODUCTION TO THE SERIES

When I first became an English teacher, there was one subject above all others that I intended to avoid: American Literature—you know, that typically junior-level English course with everything from dry Puritan writings to indecipherable Huckleberry Finn dialect. What fun. Not only did the literature fail to excite me, but as an American myself, I deemed my country's literature too close, too familiar. The stories of the rest of the world seemed more interesting and important. Yet, as it often happens in life, I found myself walking the very path I had intended to avoid. The assignment of teaching American Literature fell to me, and I reluctantly complied—knowing full well that it would be drudgery—a prediction that proved to be accurate during that first year teaching it. I chalked this defeat up to the subject matter and resolved to avoid it in the future whenever possible.

When the opportunity (demand) came to teach American Literature again a few years later, the prospect of more drudgery forced me to re-evaluate. Maybe the content was not the problem. Maybe I was. Perhaps my students hadn't been engaged in the subject matter because *I* hadn't been engaged.

Sometimes in order to be a better teacher, you must become a better student. So the next time around I resolved to become a better student of the literature. I tried harder, I dug deeper, and in doing so I made a breakthrough. I developed a true passion for teaching American Literature.

As it turns out, the reasons I had first derided American Literature were actually some of its biggest assets. It was familiar, yes, but also applicable. (Anything students learn about their own country is something they can immediately apply.) The literature I had written off as simple and underdeveloped was actually complex and challenging—not to mention vital to the development of the country I call home. How could I not teach it?

What hooked me most the second time through was the realization that the United States of America began as an experiment—a balancing act of ideas and beliefs that barely received a chance to exist in the first place. Even today America is still a country locked in a constant struggle to hold true to its values while still extending itself toward new challenges. The experiment continues.

At many points in American history, the experiment seemed doomed to fail, yet it survived—miraculously. Along the way, as America survived more obstacles, the country became more defined and developed a national identity. The literature of America is a map of this process, a record of our country's development. At times the literature was simply a reflection of national struggles, and at other times it was actually a catalyst for those struggles, but at all times the literature was there—pushing America to become better. Key fiction and non-fiction pieces helped shape what it means to be an American.

In our time it seems that America is again facing an identity crisis. Some look to the past and say we have forgotten what made America great in the first place. Others look to the future and say America must change to meet the demands of the future. I posit that both sides are correct. The balancing act continues.

Where will our young people fit in? Well, they are the future, so they must be educated—prepared to face the future problems of America. As an English teacher, I must teach them the only way I know how: showing them how America has defined and redefined itself through its literature. In essence I am not just teaching American Literature; I am attempting to create better U.S. citizens through a better understanding of America itself—what it meant then and what it means now.

My tool for this lofty quest is the American Dream, the thread that runs through all American Literature. This dream was there from the very beginning, and it progressed from era to era, adapting itself to new challenges and concerns. Pilgrims and pioneers built their lives upon it. Great leaders enshrined it in law. Wars tested and tried it. Outcasts expanded its reach. Crises questioned its validity. New generations revived it and adopted it—making it their own. This dream is not only for the past but also the future. As I teach the American Dream, I encourage my students to embrace it for themselves in order to build their own lives and enrich their future. The dream lives on through them, and the experiment continues.

Certain texts have emerged as the "great works" in American Literature. While these works can be debated, vilified, and debased, they endure as great works for a reason: They capture the successes and failures of the American Dream in their own time period. Yet many of these texts are missing from most classrooms simply because they are inaccessible or indecipherable to the average high-school student. In order to immerse my students in a thorough survey of American Literature, I had to find a way for them to experience many important texts from America's past in a single course. I turned to a classroom technique that I had found successful before: Reader's Theater script-stories. This technique allows me to streamline the literature and better engage my students in a full-class learning experience. As another strategy, I use as much history as possible to round out the literature. To me history and literature are two sides of the same coin. History grounds literature in reality, while literature gives history a voice. Have I been successful? Over the years my students have responded well to the literature, thought deeply about its connection to America's development, and written introspectively about what their country means to them. Have I equipped them to be the next stewards of America? Only time will tell.

In the *Searching for America* series you will find the script-stories, which I have used to adapt many important fiction and non-fiction texts from American Literature. I have done my best to preserve the author's intent and style, while still making their works more accessible to modern learners. Like me I hope you will see American Literature as an enjoyable and important subject to teach. Let's do all we can to make sure the grand experiment of America continues to succeed.

USING THIS BOOK IN THE CLASSROOM

Script-stories (also known as Reader's Theater) are a highly motivational learning strategy that blends oral reading, literature, and drama. Unlike traditional theater, script-stories do not require costumes, make-up, props, stage sets, or memorization. Only the script and a healthy imagination are needed. As students read the script aloud, they interpret the emotions, beliefs, attitudes, and motives of the characters. A narrator conveys the story's setting and action and provides the commentary necessary for the transitions between scenes.

While Reader's Theater has been enormously successful with lower grade-levels, it is a great fit for older learners as well. Students of any age enjoy and appreciate the chance to *experience* a story rather than having it read to them. For years now script-stories have been my secret weapon for teaching literature to high-schoolers. I wouldn't have it any other way.

The following are answers to some of the most frequently asked questions concerning the use of script-stories in the classroom:

How do you stage these stories in the classroom? Hand out photocopies of the particular script for that day. (Note: It is perfectly legal for you to photocopy pages from this book. That is what it was designed for!) To make things run more smoothly, certain copies of the scripts should be highlighted for particular characters, so that whichever students you pick to read parts will have their lines readily available. Some teachers who use Reader's Theater require their students to stand when reading their lines or even incorporate physical acting, but I do not. This should be your own preference. As for the sound effects in the plays (*fanfare*), noisemakers can be distributed to the students and used when prompted. Otherwise, students can make the noises with their own voices.

How do you structure a class around script-stories? How often do you use them? Too much of a good thing can be bad. In my own classroom I do employ the script-stories frequently—in some units we read three or four scripts a week—but I do supplement them with silent reading, notes, classroom activities, and self-created worksheets. Some of these activities appear in the in the back of the textbook and others are posted at my website: *www.creativeenglishteacher.com*.

How do you assess script-stories? A quick reading quiz after the completion of a script is an easy way to assess comprehension. In my own classroom I ask five questions that hit the high-points of the story. Each script in this book comes with five recall questions for this purpose.

A technique for informal assessment is classroom discussion. How well students discuss will tell you how well they have comprehended the story. The discussion questions included in this book have seen success in my own classroom.

I hope you find this book to be a great resource. It was designed with the intent of helping a much wider audience experience timeless tales in a new manner. Below I have listed some further notes concerning the script-stories. Thanks for purchasing this book. Please feel free to contact me if you have any questions.

Sincerely,

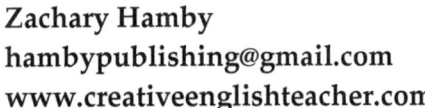

Zachary Hamby
hambypublishing@gmail.com
www.creativeenglishteacher.com

FURTHER NOTES FOR TEACHERS

UNIT PLAN The script-stories in this book are organized in the order in which they should be read. The stories range between 25-45 minutes in length. Teaching one a day and including some of the suggested activities (see individual teacher pages) should yield at least an 11-day unit. Supplemental activities from the back can be inserted as well. For even more information on setting up a unit using these scripts, visit my website, *creativeenglishteacher.com*, where sample course outlines are available.

INTENDED AUDIENCE: 6th-12th grade

LENGTH: Script-stories range between 25-45 minutes in length

SCRIPT-STORY PROCESS

- Every student will need a copy of the script-story.
- Reading parts may be highlighted for greater reading ease.
- As the teacher, you are the casting director. Assign the parts as you deem best.
- Give your largest parts to your strongest readers but still try to draw out the reluctant participant.
- As the teacher, you should take the part of the narrator. Actively participating only makes it more fun for you and the students.
- Cut loose and have fun. Script-stories allow students to see their teacher in a whole new light.

POSSIBLE MODIFICATIONS

- Costumes, props, and even sets can be added to any script-story to make it more engaging.
- Requiring the students to stand while reading their parts creates a stronger dynamic between speaking roles.
- Encouraging students to write their own script-stories gets them thinking about the elements of storytelling and the use of dialogue.
- Assigning one student to be responsible for all the sound effects in a script can involve someone who is not a strong reader in the performance. Including certain tools that actually make the indicated sound effects (noise-makers, coconuts, etc.) is another excellent way to add interest.

American Dreamers: An Introduction for Students 11

AMERICAN DREAMERS

In the pages of history the United States of America is exceptional. Many have tried to pinpoint the secret of its success. To find the spirit of America—to know what makes it tick, what makes it unique—one must look into the past—in the ambitions of its first citizens, the events of its formation, and the dreams of its greatest leaders.

While other nations formed haphazardly or almost accidentally, America was the first nation founded on an idea—and not just any idea, the monumental idea that all men are created equal. The nation became a Grand Experiment conducted by honorable leaders who loved liberty more than life. However, it was not a nation without its struggles. Throughout the centuries, this experimental nation faced conflicts, which tested the principles upon which it was founded. At many points it was not clear whether or not a nation built for the people and by the people could long endure. Yet it did endure, against all odds, and continues to this day.

As you study America's past, you will encounter something called "The American Dream," and unless you understand this dream, you will fail to grasp America's greatness. Why did men, women, and children travel great distances, suffer great hardships, and even offer up their lives to create and preserve this dream? The answer is simple: To exercise and ensure the rights that we now enjoy. Through studying their journeys and reading their words, you will hear your own hopes echoed in theirs. Like you they desired the opportunity to live life free, to build their lives, and fulfill their potential.

To dream, to hope are two things that are uniquely American. According to James Truslow Adams, the historian who first coined the phrase "The American Dream," our country would not have made a unique contribution to history if it had not been for the American Dream. In his book *The Epic of America*, Adams stated that this "dream of a land in which life should be richer and fuller for every man" with "opportunity for each [person] according to ability" was a gift to all mankind. The idea that every man and woman could "be recognized by others for what they are" regardless of their position in society not only revolutionized *our* country, but the whole world. Adams ended with a warning that we should never become weary or mistrustful of this unique Dream of ours, but embrace it wholeheartedly.

The American Dream is still around today. For some it means financial security and professional success. For others it means equality and religious freedom. The genius of the American Dream is that it is both universal and personal—every American should have one, but no two need be alike.

All that America was is still alive—and will only remain so as long as its citizens remember the spirit of its greatness. As you read the words in this book, written by men and women long dead, do not forget that many of them achieved goals that others said were impossible. Then think of your own dreams. Where will your life, liberty, and pursuit of happiness take you? Do not squander the opportunity you have been given. Dare to dream.

THE FLYING CANOE
TEACHER GUIDE

BACKGROUND

When the first European explorers arrived in the New World, they found it already inhabited by a native people with a culture far different than their own. The Native Americans (or American Indians as they were called) fascinated the Europeans and vice versa; however, rather than seeking to understand one another and co-exist peacefully, native and European leaders tried to exploit the other side to their advantage. This lack of understanding between the two cultures led to much heartbreak, abuse, and division in the following centuries.

Although the numerous Native American tribes share common elements, many have their own unique languages, cultures, and myths. The two myths included here originate from the Northeastern portion of the United States, where the first English settlers arrived. These script-stories are merely adaptations of the myths, and some liberties have been taken to adapt the stories.

SUMMARY

Joseph is a young Indian warrior, who is always at the mercy of his older, fiercely-competitive brothers. One day a strange, old woman wanders out of the forest and begs for the villagers to give her shelter and food. When none of the others help her, Joseph offers her hospitality. In return for his kindness the woman tells Joseph the following story about the creation of the world.

The world was once covered in water, and all the birds hovered over it. One day the birds saw a woman falling from the sky and knew she was the wife of the Sky-holder. Working together, they caught her with their wings and kept her from falling into the water; however, the birds saw that there was no place for her to land, so they summoned the Great Tortoise from the depths of the water. Rising up, his shell gave the woman dry land. So today all dry land rests upon the back of that Great Tortoise. Then the sky-woman gave birth to twin sons—one was the Spirit of Good and one was the Spirit of Evil.

The old woman explains to Joseph that part of the Spirit of Good is in him and part of the Spirit of Evil is in his brothers, so she will help him get the best of his brothers. Joseph also loves a maiden named Blue Flower and hopes to win her heart. Before the wise woman can help Joseph each time he asks, she asks first to be fed. After she has eaten, the old woman tells Joseph to cut down a tree and carve a pair of wooden moccasins from it. Joseph does so, and these wooden shoes give him the power to run faster than his brothers; however, he foolishly tells his brothers how he created the shoes, and they create pairs for themselves.

In anger Joseph returns to the wise woman and demands that she help him again. This time she tells him to cut down a tree and build a dugout canoe from it. When he does so, Joseph's canoe is faster than his brothers', but they guess his secret and make fast canoes for themselves from the same tree.

In frustration Joseph asks the wise woman to help him again. Before she does, she tells him a story about the origin of corn—how a yellow-haired woman was created for the first man. This woman commanded her husband to drag her by her hair across scorched earth, and this caused the first corn to grow.

The wise woman tells Joseph that she will enchant his canoe so that it will fly. Joseph jumps into his flying canoe and goes on many adventures in faraway lands. On these adventures Joseph learns an important lesson—he truly loves and misses his brothers. When Joseph returns, he makes peace with his brothers and finds that Blue Flower is willing to be his wife—not because he is the strongest or the fastest but because she loved him all along.

ESSENTIAL QUESTIONS

- Is being competitive good or bad?
- Should you change yourself in order to get someone else to like you?

CONNECT

Nature and Creation Among the varied Indians tribes of America, there are countless tales of how the world began. Research several of these and compare them to one another. Identify some common elements in the stories.

ANTICIPATORY QUESTIONS

- What do you know about Native American culture?
- Are brothers and sisters naturally competitive?
- Would you enjoy having super speed?

TEACHABLE TERMS

- **Frame Story** The initial story of Joseph competing against his brothers serves as a frame story for two shorter stories—one that tells of the origin of the earth and the other that explains the origin of corn.
- **Imagery/Simile** On pg. 16 the author uses imagery and two similes to describe the wise woman: "Her skin was as brown as the earth, and her hair as tangled as tree roots."
- **Archetype** The archetype of the old, wise woman who seems to have magical powers is a common archetype in many Native American myths. Compare this character type to wise mentor figures in other stories you have heard.
- **Characterization** The quality that sets Joseph apart from his selfish brothers is his kindness and generosity. On pg. 16 the wise woman points this out to Joseph when she tells him, "You have little, that is true, but you are willing to share it. And that makes all the difference."
- **Ambiguity** Whether or not the wise woman is the supernatural sky-woman who appears in the creation story is left unclear, even when Joseph asks her directly on pg. 22. Examine how this ambiguity adds some mystery to the story.

RECALL QUESTIONS

1. What does the wise woman ask Joseph to do for her before she will help him?
2. What is the first magical item the wise woman allows Joseph to have?
3. According to the creation myth in this story, dry land was formed from what?
4. According to another myth in this story, how was corn created?
5. What magical object allows Joseph to go on many adventures?

THE FLYING CANOE

CAST

JOSEPH	*Young Man*
BLUE FLOWER	*Lovely Maiden*
BROTHER ONE	*Joseph's Older Brother*
BROTHER TWO	*Joseph's Older Brother*
WISE WOMAN	*Crippled, Old Woman*
BIRD ONE	*Bird of the Air*
BIRD TWO	*Bird of the Air*
MONSTER	*Creature of the Deep*
TORTOISE	*Enormous Turtle*
MAN	*Lonely Man*
GOLD WOMAN	*Mysterious Woman*

NARRATOR: In a village there lived three brothers, who were all fiercely competitive. The two oldest brothers were brawny warriors, the best at everything—running, hunting, fishing—while the youngest, Joseph, was not.

BROTHER ONE: Joseph, what a weakling you are! Even the feeblest man in the village is stronger than you!

BROTHER TWO: Even the women are stronger than him!

BROTHER ONE: If I were you, I would not show my face outside my lodge.

JOSEPH: Leave me alone. One day you will see. One day you will see how strong I am.

NARRATOR: But in his heart, Joseph almost despaired. He felt there was no way he could be the equal of his brothers—let alone their better.

Among the girls of the tribe was a girl named Blue Flower. Although she had reached the age of marriage, she had not given any of the young warriors an indication that she was interested in him.

BROTHER ONE: Please, Blue Flower! Choose me as your husband! Look at how often I bring home a mighty kill.

BROTHER TWO: Ignore him, Blue Flower. Choose me instead. No one can paddle a canoe as swiftly as I can.

BROTHER ONE: Butt out!

BROTHER TWO: Make me!

(sounds of a scuffle)

NARRATOR: Blue Flower smiled. That was all she ever did when men offered to be her husband

Like all the other men of the village, Joseph longed for Blue Flower, but he never had the courage to speak to her. Yet when she happened to be passing his way, she would smile and say hello to him.

BLUE FLOWER: Hello, Joseph.

JOSEPH: H-h-hello, Blue Flower.

NARRATOR: Once Joseph's brothers happened to spy Joseph watching Blue Flower as she ground grain.

BROTHER ONE: Ha! Look at that! Little Joseph has eyes for Blue Flower!

BROTHER TWO: Joseph, what makes you think a woman such as her would ever want a weakling such as you?

JOSEPH: Well, she obviously has no interest in the two of you.

BROTHER ONE: (angrily) Come here, you runt! We will teach you to sass us!

(sounds of a scuffle)

NARRATOR: One day a stranger hobbled into the village from the deep forest. As she passed through, all the tribe watched her uneasily. (murmuring of the villagers) She was a strange old woman, who was so gaunt she could barely walk. Her skin was as brown as the earth, and her hair as tangled as a tree roots. She hobbled from home to home—seeking anyone to give her nourishment.

WISE WOMAN: (weakly) Please, help me. I am so hungry.

BROTHER ONE: Get out of here, old woman! You are not of our tribe!

WISE WOMAN: That is true. I am from a tribe far older than yours.

BROTHER TWO: Begone, you old, crippled crone!

NARRATOR: Everyone in the village rejected her, but Joseph took pity on her.

JOSEPH: Come with me, old woman. I will show you to my lodge.

WISE WOMAN: Oh, thank you. Do you have something to eat there?

BROTHER ONE: (shouting) So, Joseph, did you finally give up on Blue Flower and pick another wife?

BROTHER TWO: Ha! Blue Flower was as fresh as a daisy. This one looks more like a dried-up husk.

BROTHER ONE: He traded Blue Flower for Brown Cornhusk! Ha-ha!

JOSEPH: Close your rude mouths before I close them for you.

NARRATOR: Joseph's brothers continued to jeer and mock him, but Blue Flower was watching, too, and she smiled at Joseph's kindness.

Joseph showed the old woman to his own lodge. There he presented her with what little food he had.

JOSEPH: I am not the best hunter, so I don't have much game. If you had been welcomed into the dwelling of my brothers, they could have offered you much more.

WISE WOMAN: But I was not welcomed there. You have little, that is true, but you are willing to share it. And that makes all the difference.

NARRATOR: As Joseph set the meat before the old woman, she fell upon it and devoured it greedily. (smacking and slurping sounds)

Joseph had never seen an old woman eat so much. She raised her shaggy head and shook it. When she did, dust fell from her hair, and her back straightened a bit.

WISE WOMAN: Go. Hunt more for me.

JOSEPH: But I just told you, I am not a good hunter.

WISE WOMAN: (*forcefully*) Go! Do as I say! I am your guest!

NARRATOR: So Joseph went reluctantly.

JOSEPH: (*grumbling*) She's certainly bossy.

NARRATOR: But for once, fortune was with him, and his hunt was successful. He brought the game back to the old woman. This, too, she greedily feasted upon. (*slurping sounds*) Many times Joseph did this—returning with more and more game—until he was exhausted.

JOSEPH: (*breathing heavily*) How much can one old woman eat?

NARRATOR: The old woman patted her stomach and wiped her mouth.

WISE WOMAN: That is fine. I am full—for now.

NARRATOR: Then she looked deeply at Joseph. Maybe it was a trick of the firelight, but the crisscrossing wrinkles upon her face seemed as deep and bottomless as dark ravines.

WISE WOMAN: For your kindness I will tell you a story.

JOSEPH: No, thank you. I am tired and—

WISE WOMAN: Sit. Listen to the story.

NARRATOR: The old woman cleared her throat and began to wave her hands through the smoke of the lodge fire. The wisps rose upward—dancing to the words of her story.

WISE WOMAN: Long ago in the great past, there were no people on the earth. All of it was covered by deep water. Flying birds filled the air, and many huge monsters possessed the waters. One day the birds looked up—high, high in the sky—and they saw a woman falling from heaven. It was the wife of the Sky-Holder.

BIRD ONE: Brawk! Look at that! We must help that poor woman! If we don't, she will fall into the water and drown.

BIRD TWO: But we are just birds—small and weak. What can we do?

BIRD ONE: We can work together.

WISE WOMAN: All the birds spread out their wings, so that their wingtips were touching and so formed a feathery cushion for the falling woman. (*Shoom!*) The sky-woman was saved from crashing down into the water.

JOSEPH: Who was the falling woman?

WISE WOMAN: The wife of the Sky-Holder—the Maker in the Sky.

JOSEPH: He must have wanted rid of her, huh? (*laugh*)

WISE WOMAN: I do not think that is funny. Now, don't interrupt. (*narrating*) The birds, carrying the sky-woman upon their wings, now had a problem.

BIRD ONE: We saved her, but what now?

BIRD TWO: We will have to hold her up forever, I guess.

BIRD ONE: Unless…

WISE WOMAN: The birds cried out to the monsters of the deep.

BIRD ONE: We have saved this sky-woman from falling into the deep waters. What can you now do to help her?

WISE WOMAN: The monsters held a council and decided they should summon the Great Tortoise.

MONSTER: *(gurgling)* Only the Great Tortoise is big enough to bear her weight.

BIRD TWO: Well, hurry and summon him! We can't hold this woman up forever!

WISE WOMAN: So the Great Tortoise was summoned from the depths. From the muddy bottoms he emerged—slowly.

(gurgling of the waters)

MONSTER: Hurry! The birds' strength cannot hold out forever!

TORTOISE: *(slowly)* Rush, rush, rush. Always in a hurry.

WISE WOMAN: The massive tortoise raised his shell out of the water, and the birds lowered the sky-woman down onto its mossy surface. Then magically the Great Tortoise began to grow. *(growing sound)*

TORTOISE: Huh? What is happening?

WISE WOMAN: The Tortoise became a large island. Then the sky-woman cried out in pain, for she had begun to give birth. *(crying of a woman)* She gave birth to twin boys. The first was the Spirit of Good. He made it possible for all the crops of the world to grow. The other twin was the Spirit of Evil. He created the weeds and also the worms and the bugs, and all other evil creatures.

TORTOISE: Ah! I feel like a stretch! Hmmm. That's better.

WISE WOMAN: The Tortoise continued to stretch, and every time he did his shell became larger and larger—until it was big enough for many tribes to live upon it. Yet when he shivered or moved too quickly, the Tortoise caused all the earth to shake. *(pause)* And that is my story. Hmmm. All that talk of birds made me hungry. Perhaps you could do some more hunting for me.

JOSEPH: Why did you tell me that story, wise woman?

WISE WOMAN: Because some of that art of the Spirit of Good is in me—and in you. And some of that twisted art of the Spirit of Evil is in your brothers. I have come to help you.

JOSEPH: Ha! What can an old woman do for me? Can you help me hunt deer and spear fish like my brothers? Can you help me win Blue Flower's heart? I must do a great deed to impress her.

WISE WOMAN: Listen to me, and I will give you all of that—and more. Go. Take your axe. Make a pair of moccasins out of wood.

JOSEPH: Wooden moccasins? What sense does that make?

WISE WOMAN: Since when does magic have to make sense? Make the shoes.

NARRATOR: So Joseph did as the old woman said. He cut down a tree and whittled himself some shoes out of the timber. *(sounds of woodworking)* Then he slipped the wooden moccasins on his feet and made his way back into the village.

BROTHER ONE: Have you been chopping wood for your new wife? Old Cornhusk seems like a slave master.

JOSEPH: No. I made myself these wooden shoes.

BROTHER TWO: You are even dumber than we thought! You'll get splinters in your toes!

NARRATOR: Yet Joseph had faith in the wise woman's words. He began to run—speeding past his amazed brothers like a flash of light. *(Zoom!)*

JOSEPH: What did you say, brothers? I was moving so fast I could not hear you!

NARRATOR: Moving like the wind, he sped into the forest, caught a mighty stag in his grip, bound it with leather strips, and carried back to the village in the blink of an eye. His brothers stared at him in shock.

BROTHER TWO: Wha—?

JOSEPH: You're speechless I see. That is a first.

BROTHER ONE: H-h-how did you—?

JOSEPH: I guess I am not as foolish as you thought, brothers. Perhaps you should try splinters in *your* toes sometimes.

NARRATOR: Joseph heaved the bound stag onto his brothers, who collapsed under its weight. *(sound of a crash and groaning from the brothers)* Joseph returned to the wise woman and told her of his newfound speed.

WISE WOMAN: Good. Good. I am glad you are happy. But I am afraid it will be short-lived.

JOSEPH: What? How could I ever be sad again? I'm the fastest warrior in the village. I am the fastest warrior anywhere!

NARRATOR: Meanwhile, Joseph's angry brothers were trying to figure out his secret.

BROTHER ONE: Where did Joseph get such speed?

BROTHER TWO: It must be those shoes! Where did he get them?

NARRATOR: The brothers found the spot where Joseph had carved his moccasins. There was part of the log Joseph had used and wood chips scattered upon the ground.

BROTHER TWO: There must be magic in this. We should carve our own shoes out of the same wood. Then we will be as fast as Joseph.

NARRATOR: The next time Joseph went for a hunt, speeding along the ground twice as quickly as the swiftest deer, he heard a sound growing louder behind him. It was his brothers, wearing their own wooden shoes.

JOSEPH: Impossible!

NARRATOR: Then with a burst of speed, they sped past him. *(Shoom!)*

BROTHER ONE: Ha! We know your trick! Now we are just as swift as you!

BROTHER TWO: Don't try to beat us again, brother.

NARRATOR: Joseph returned to the wise woman and threw the wooden moccasins down at her feet.

WISE WOMAN: Unhappy? *(sarcastically)* I thought you would be happy forever.

JOSEPH: My brothers made moccasins just like mine! I thought you said the magic was just for me!

WISE WOMAN: You did not guard your secret. Your brothers have the Spirit of Evil in them. They take what is good and use it for their own purposes. I will give you another trick. This time, keep it secret. But first feed me.

NARRATOR: Joseph went into the wood and caught much more food for the withered old woman.

WISE WOMAN: Mmmm. So tasty!

JOSEPH: How can you eat so much?

WISE WOMAN: Working magic really takes it out of me! Now, go make a dugout canoe for yourself. It will speed across the water faster than any bird.

NARRATOR: So Joseph began the process in secret—doing all his work at night. He fell a tree and shaved off the bark. Then he began to dig out the interior. Finally his canoe was done. He took it out on the water to test it out, and the old woman was right. It flew across the water like a bird. *(Zip!)*

JOSEPH: Ha-ha! With this I will be able to chase down the fastest whale!

NARRATOR: But Joseph did not know that his brothers had been spying on him. They took the part of the tree that he had not used and all his wood chips and made their own canoe. Since they worked together, it was even better than his.

Joseph had paddled downriver and made his way out into the sea when he saw his brothers' canoe gaining on him. Joseph despaired as his brothers sped past him.

BROTHER ONE: The hunt is ours! We are off to spear whales!

BROTHER TWO: Didn't we warn you? You can never beat us, brother! Give up!

NARRATOR: Joseph went back to the wise woman full of anger.

JOSEPH: Once again they have beaten me!

WISE WOMAN: Such competition will only lead to disappointment. Why do you care who is the fastest or the strongest?

JOSEPH: I care because—because Blue Flower cares.

WISE WOMAN: Are you sure? Have you asked her?

JOSEPH: All girls want the man who is the fastest and the strongest.

WISE WOMAN: Hmmm. Perhaps she wants the man who will love her the most deeply. Let me tell you another story.

JOSEPH: Right now? My brothers will soon be hauling whales back to our village, and you want to tell me a story?

NARRATOR: The old woman pursed her withered lips at the young man.

WISE WOMAN: Sit. Listen. Learn.

NARRATOR: Joseph reluctantly complied.

WISE WOMAN: First, I told you of the making of the world. But here is what happened next. When the Great Sky-Holder looked down and saw the world's barrenness, he made man to fill it. Out of all these men, one man lived apart, and he lived a wretched existence—because he did not have good things to eat.

JOSEPH: Everything is food with you, isn't it?

WISE WOMAN: It is. Now be quiet. *(narrating)* Like I was saying, all he had to eat was roots, bark, and nuts. Squirrel food. And he was lonely, too. So the Sky-Holder sent him a present—a woman. Her hair was long and golden. The man was overcome with passion.

MAN: *(passionately)* Whoever you are, beautiful one, you must be mine!

WISE WOMAN: But the golden-haired woman only smiled.

GOLD WOMAN: I will be yours only if you do exactly as I say.

WISE WOMAN: First, she told the man to take two dry sticks and rub them together over a clump of dry grass. When he did, fire sprang up.

MAN: What is this magic?

WISE WOMAN: The fire burned away all the dry grass in the field before him. Then the golden-haired woman spoke to him again.

GOLD WOMAN: When the sun sets, you must take me by the hair and drag me over the burned ground.

MAN: *(in shock)* What? Pull your beautiful hair? But I love you! Never! Never!

GOLD WOMAN: If you love me, you will do what I say. Then I will be able to bless you.

WISE WOMAN: Even though it broke his heart, the man took the woman by the hair and dragged her back and forth over the burnt ground. As he did, something like grass sprang up behind her. Between the leaves grew out fibers like hair—hair as golden as the woman's.

GOLD WOMAN: Now watch them grow.

WISE WOMAN: The leaves grew up into stalks and tasseled out. The ears of corn produced silks, which resembled the woman's hair.

GOLD WOMAN: Now, I will be your wife. You listened to me, and I was able to give you a great gift.

WISE WOMAN: Today when our people see the silks on a corn stalk, they remember that first wife who blessed her husband. They know the golden-haired woman will be with them forever.

JOSEPH: Let me see. You told me that story to show me the blessing that a wife can be.

WISE WOMAN: Yes, but telling it made me hungry for corn. You don't have any, do you?

JOSEPH: Old woman, I will give you all the corn in the world if you can help me win Blue Flower and beat my brothers!

WISE WOMAN: Very well. I have promised that I will help. But you must listen to me! *(growling stomach)* Oooh. If you want more help, you will have to find me more food! My stomach aches.

NARRATOR: So Joseph gave the old woman more food than ever before. Her stomach bulged out from the rest of her withered body.

WISE WOMAN: I will do something greater than ever before, but it may not be what you hoped for.

JOSEPH: How could it not be what I hoped for? Help me get the better of my brothers! Help me win Blue Flower!

NARRATOR: The old woman reached out her withered hand and placed it upon his chest.

WISE WOMAN: Your brothers are not your enemies. You will realize that in time.

NARRATOR: Joseph looked into the depths of the old woman's eyes. The further he looked into them, the deeper they took him—swimming back through the years. It made Joseph tremble with awe.

WISE WOMAN: I will help you—not because of what you hope to gain but because of the lesson you will learn from it.

JOSEPH: *(breathlessly)* Who are you, wise woman? Are you the woman who fell out of the sky?

NARRATOR: The old woman laughed.

WISE WOMAN: *(laugh)* If I were, why would I tell you that?

NARRATOR: She removed her hand from him, and it was as if he was released from a spell.

WISE WOMAN: I will give you the greatest canoe that has ever been made.

JOSEPH: It cannot be better than the one my brothers have created.

WISE WOMAN: Really? Can theirs fly?

JOSEPH: Fly? *(laughs)* Fantastic! They could never compete with that.

NARRATOR: Joseph could not contain his excitement. He ran out to where his canoe was pulled up onto the riverbank, and he jumped inside of it. As soon as he raised his paddle, the canoe itself lifted off the ground and soared into the heavens. *(Shoom!)*

JOSEPH: *(whooping)* Wah-hoo! Wah-hoo!

NARRATOR: Spying his brothers in the village below, Joseph turned the canoe and swooped down upon them. *(Shoom!)*

BROTHER ONE: *(cry of fright)* Ah! What is that?

BROTHER TWO: It's—it's—Joseph!

JOSEPH: See, brothers? I told you one day you would know my strength! Now, I am off to have adventures that you can only ever dream about!

NARRATOR: The flying canoe lifted Joseph high up over the village, over the treetops, and then over the hills. Then he was gone.

The old wise woman, who now had no one to care for her, was offered a place in the lodge of Blue Flower.

BLUE FLOWER: Grandmother, you are welcome to live with my family. If Joseph was kind to you, I will be kind to you as well.

WISE WOMAN: Thank you. *(pause)* Do you have anything to eat?

NARRATOR: After Joseph's disappearance, his brothers were quite changed men. They did not boast or brag as they had before. They had seen something that they had never seen before—that they loved and missed their little brother. Their gaze would often stray to the top of the hills where Joseph had vanished—hoping to see the return of the flying canoe.

Months passed. Then one day as the old wise woman was sitting in the lodge of Blue Flower all alone, she heard a gentle noise outside. It was the sound of a keel scraping over solid ground.

WISE WOMAN: Joseph, you have come back.

NARRATOR: Joseph stepped through the doorway. He was different. He looked older and wiser. A cloak was thrown around his shoulders—one far different than the dress of his tribe.

WISE WOMAN: What all did you see?

JOSEPH: I saw far off places—and strange people. I had many adventures. But I could not stop thinking of my home—my brothers and Blue Flower. Everything seemed so meaningless without them.

NARRATOR: The old woman smiled.

WISE WOMAN: Then you have learned a bit of wisdom.

JOSEPH: How are my brothers? I feel so foolish for how I acted before. Are they well?

WISE WOMAN: They are well. Once they were sick. But they have been healed.

JOSEPH: Thank you—thank you for helping me.

WISE WOMAN: You? I did not come to help just you.

JOSEPH: What about Blue Flower? Do you think she will want me now that I am a great warrior and an adventurer?

WISE WOMAN: No.

JOSEPH: *(in shock)* What?

WISE WOMAN: I think she will want you because you are Joseph and she is Blue Flower.

JOSEPH: But I went all over the world trying to win her heart.

WISE WOMAN: You went to find something that was already yours.

JOSEPH: Then all of this has been for nothing.

WISE WOMAN: No. You have learned. And nothing is wasted when a lesson is learned.

JOSEPH: Thank you, wise woman.

WISE WOMAN: Now, after all your travels, I must ask you—what did you bring me to eat?

NARRATOR: So Joseph was wed to Blue Flower and made peace with his brothers. The old wise woman stayed long enough for his marriage feast and ate more than all the other villagers put together. Then waddling a bit, she slipped back into the woods and was seen no more.

DISCUSSION QUESTIONS

1. What lesson or lessons does Joseph learn in this story?
2. What is interesting about the way the Native Americans in this story describe the creation of the earth?
3. What do you find interesting about the creation of corn?
4. Based on this story, what are some details you can infer about Native American culture?
5. What do you think is the true identity of the old woman?

GLUSCABI
TEACHER GUIDE

BACKGROUND

Gluscabi (gloo-skah-bee), also known as Glooscap, is a trickster character from the mythology of the Wabanaki, native peoples located in Maine and Atlantic Canada. Gluscabi's many misadventures illustrate a principle central to Native American culture—the balance of nature. Since Indian tribes existed off the bounty of the land, this fragile balance was sacred. Abusing nature would lead to its inability to sustain the ones who depended on it the most. In this story, which combines three different myths, Gluscabi learns to respect the balance of nature and battle others who try to violate it.

The American Indians spoke of their relationship to the earth in terms of family. To them the earth was not something to be bought and sold. It was, quite simply, their mother. And the rest of creation, all around them, shared in that family relationship. All living things had a spirit and were worthy of respect. In fact, as their stories show, humans and animals are basically interchangeable (for example, Gluscabi's guardian, Grandmother Woodchuck). The Indians did not see themselves as rulers of creation, but as keepers of the earth.

SUMMARY

When Tabaldak, the Creator or "Owner," first creates man, he brushes the excess dust from his hands. From this dust the creature Gluscabi creates himself. Because of this, Gluscabi possesses some of the Owner's power to change things. Since Gluscabi does not look like the other human beings, he is forced to live apart from them with an animal guardian, Grandmother Woodchuck.

Since Gluscabi sees hunting game for his food each day as exhausting work, he asks Grandmother Woodchuck to make him a large game bag. The size that he requests is so large that Grandmother Woodchuck runs out of deer hair to make it, so she plucks out some of her own belly hair to complete it. This explains why woodchucks have no hair on their bellies. Then Gluscabi tricks all the animals of the forest to run into the game bag by telling them that the world is ending. Although Gluscabi thinks he will never have to hunt again, Grandmother Woodchuck scolds him—telling him that now all the animals will die and there will be no more to hunt. Gluscabi sees the error of his way and releases them.

Gluscabi's next adventure occurs when he is angered by the fiercely blowing wind. He follows the wind for many days until he reaches Grandfather Wuchosen, the wind-eagle whose wings power the winds. Here the winds are so fierce that they blow off Glusabi's shoes, clothes, and even his hair. Hoping to end the violent winds, Gluscabi tricks the wind-eagle by offering to carry him to a higher mountain peak. When the eagle agrees, Gluscabi binds the eagle's wings and tosses him into a crevice. However, once Gluscabi returns home and sees how nature has changed because of the wind's absence, he returns to the mountain and frees the eagle.

Finally, Gluscabi learns of a water monster that has dammed a nearby river—depriving a tribe of its water source. Gluscabi decides to use his powers for good and faces the water monster, defeating it and shrinking it down into a bullfrog. This explains why bullfrogs still croak at anyone who tries to share their water. By the end of the story

Gluscabi has finally learned the lesson of respecting nature.

ESSENTIAL QUESTIONS

- How can we use our abilities for good rather than evil?
- Why is the balance of nature important?

CONNECT

Native Languages Several Abenaki-Penobscot words and phrases are incorporated into this script-story. *Oleohneh* (O-lee-o-nay) means "thank you." *Kaamoji* (Kah-mo-gee) is an exclamation. *Ki yo wah ji neh* (kee-yo-wah-gee-nay) is a line from Gluscabi's rowing song, but the literal meaning is unknown.

ANTICIPATORY QUESTIONS

- Why is the balance of nature important?
- Have you ever wondered why the world works the way it does?
- Have you ever thought you were doing the right thing only to learn later that you were making a mistake?

TEACHABLE TERMS

- **Archetype** The trickster is a common archetype (or character type) in many myths from around the world. Tricksters often impact the world in both harmful and helpful ways. Examine the ways that Gluscabi is a trickster.
- **Theme** Examine how the balance of nature is developed as a theme in the story.
- **Dynamic Character** Examine how Gluscabi's adventures change him from a violator of the laws of nature to a protector of the laws of nature and explain why this qualifies him as a dynamic character.
- **Hyperbole** Extravagant exaggeration often appears in Native American myths to enhance the story by adding a sense of wonder. Examples from this story are the wind blowing off Gluscabi's hair on pg. 30, the immense size of the water monster on pg. 35, and the sudden shrinking of the water monster and the growth of Gluscabi on pg. 35.
- **Myth** A myth is an ancient story used to explain why nature functions as it does. Examples in this story are the reason why woodchucks have hairless bellies on pg. 28, the explanation of how the wind blows on pg. 30, and the creation of the first bullfrog on pg. 35.

RECALL QUESTIONS

1. How was Gluscabi created?
2. How does Gluscabi capture all the woodland animals?
3. According to the story, why do woodchucks have no hair on their bellies?
4. Who or what does Gluscabi bind and throw into a mountain ravine?
5. Gluscabi transforms a monster into what type of real-life creature?

GLUSCABI

CAST

GLUSCABI	Self-Created Creature
TABALDAK	Creator God
WOODCHUCK	Guardian of Gluscabi
RACCOON	Woodland Creature
BEAR	Woodland Creature
TURTLE	Woodland Creature
WUCHOWSEN	Giant Eagle
CHIEF	Leader of a Tribe
MAN	Man of the Tribe
WARRIOR	Warrior of the Tribe
GUARD	Tall, Fearsome Monster
MONSTER	Terrifying Creature

NARRATOR: In the beginning, after Tabaldak, the Owner, had finished making human beings, he dusted off his hands, and some of that dust fell down upon the earth. Out of the pile of dust, there crawled a creature.

TABALDAK: Who—or what—are you?

GLUSCABI: I am Gluscabi.

TABALDAK: Where did you come from? I did not create you.

GLUSCABI: I know. I created myself from this leftover dust here.

TABALDAK: If you created yourself, no wonder you look like that.

GLUSCABI: I must be ugly then.

TABALDAK: You are different. But you are wonderful.

GLUSCABI: I am wonderful because I came from the dust you sprinkled.

TABALDAK: Good answer. Let me show you the world I have made. And then I will find a home for you.

NARRATOR: So Gluscabi came into being—as a leftover creation. He was not as powerful as the Owner, but he possessed some of his power to change things. And change things he did—sometimes not for the best.
Since Gluscabi looked so different from the other humans, they would not accept him. So he went to live among the animals. An old woodchuck took him into her lodge to live as her son.

WOODCHUCK: *(chittering)* You can live here, Gluscabi, but you must not cause any trouble. You have great power, but I do not want you to use it for ill.

GLUSCABI: Of course not, Grandmother.

WOODCHUCK: You must do chores if you live here. Each day I need you to go out and hunt wild game.

GLUSCABI: Everyday? What if I do not feel like it?

WOODCHUCK: Gluscabi! If we do not hunt, we do not survive.

GLUSCABI: *(sigh)* Fine.

NARRATOR: So each day Gluscabi grudgingly went out to hunt, but he did not enjoy it. After the animal was killed, he had to drag it back home in a game sack Grandmother Woodchuck had made for him. The whole process was exhausting.

GLUSCABI: I hate hunting!

NARRATOR: But then Gluscabi had a brilliant idea—a way for him to fulfill his obligations and not waste so much effort.

GLUSCABI: Grandmother Woodchuck, I want you to make me a bigger game bag—the biggest one ever made!

NARRATOR: So Grandmother Woodchuck took deer hair and began to weave Gluscabi a bigger game bag. But each time she showed it to him, he was not satisfied with it.

GLUSCABI: No! No! No! It must be bigger!

WOODCHUCK: Bigger than that? All right.

NARRATOR: She kept sewing and sewing, and at last she ran out of hair.

GLUSCABI: That's not big enough.

WOODCHUCK: I can't make it any bigger. I have run out of hair.

GLUSCABI: Then use some of yours. That will make it even more special.

WOODCHUCK: Very well. *(plucking hair)* Ouch! Ouch!

NARRATOR: So Grandmother Woodchuck pulled out much of her belly hair in order to finish the bag. To this day woodchucks have no hair on their bellies. Then she showed the bag to her adopted son.

WOODCHUCK: There! The biggest game bag ever made! And I even enchanted it, so that you can put as much game in there as you want.

GLUSCABI: Ha! Perfect! Oleohneh, Grandmother.

NARRATOR: So Gluscabi ran through the forest as swift as an arrow. He stopped on a high hill and called out using his powerful lungs.

GLUSCABI: Listen to me, all you animals! I bring terrible news! The world and everything in it is going to be destroyed!

BEAR: Who is that? Gluscabi? What is he saying?

TURTLE: *(slowly)* The earth is going to be destroyed!

RACCOON: What can we do?

GLUSCABI: I can offer you safety! Just climb into this magical bag I have made. Then you will be safe when the world ends!

RACCOON: You don't have to tell me twice.

BEAR: Out of my way! Me first!

TURTLE: Hey! Wait up!

(thundering stampeding of the animals)

NARRATOR: All the animals of the forest crammed inside Gluscabi's bag—all thrashing against one another.

GLUSCABI: Heh heh. Suckers.

NARRATOR: The game bag was monstrously heavy, but Gluscabi managed to drag it home.

GLUSCABI: Look, Grandmother! Look!

WOODCHUCK: What on earth have you put into that bag?

GLUSCABI: All the game animals in the forest. Now I won't have to go out and hunt each day. We can just come to the bag and draw out one we want to eat.

WOODCHUCK: You foolish boy! The animals will die in that bag. They need the forest to live! Then when they all die out, where will we be? There will be no animals for our children or grandchildren to hunt.

GLUSCABI: Uhh…I did not think of that.

WOODCHUCK: You did not think at all!

GLUSCABI: But hunting is so difficult.

WOODCHUCK: That is the way of the world! The Owner planned it that way. Hunting is hard, but it will make you stronger. And the animals will also grow stronger and wiser to avoid being caught. Then things will be in the right balance.

GLUSCABI: *(sigh)* Kaamoji, Grandmother. You are right—as usual.

NARRATOR: So Gluscabi released all the animals of the woods and apologized for deceiving them.

WOODCHUCK: There is great power in you, Gluscabi. Always use it for good instead of evil.

NARRATOR: In spite of this warning Gluscabi did not listen. His next misadventure occurred one day soon after when he went out onto the bay to hunt some ducks. As he rowed his canoe out over the water, he sang a rowing song.

GLUSCABI: *(singing)*
Ki yo wah ji neh
Yo ho hey ho
Ki yo wah ji neh
Ki yo wah ji neh

NARRATOR: But suddenly the wind rose up against him fiercely. *(whooshing of the wind)* It blew so fiercely that it forced his canoe back to the shore.

GLUSCABI: I am Gluscabi! I will not be thwarted by a bit of wind.

NARRATOR: So he sang his paddling song even louder and paddled with all his might.

GLUSCABI: *(singing more loudly)*
Ki yo wah ji neh
Yo ho hey ho
Ki yo wah ji neh
Ki yo wah ji neh.

NARRATOR: But the wind blew even harder and whisked him back to shore even more quickly. Gluscabi angrily climbed out of his canoe and marched back to the lodge of Grandmother Woodchuck.

GLUSCABI: Grandmother! Grandmother!

WOODCHUCK: *(sigh)* What is it now?

GLUSCABI: Where does the wind come from?

WOODCHUCK: *(chittering)* Oh no! When you ask questions like that, it makes me so nervous! *(sigh)* But I know you will not stop asking until I tell you. Far from here on top of the tallest mountain, perches a great bird. This bird is named Wuchowsen, and when he flaps his wings, he makes the wind.

GLUSCABI: Ah-ha! And how do I find this bird?

WOODCHUCK: *(sigh)* I know I shouldn't tell you…but if you walk always facing the wind, you will finally come to the place he stands.

GLUSCABI: Perfect. Then I am off.

WOODCHUCK: To do what?

GLUSCABI: Nothing. Goodbye!

NARRATOR: Gluscabi stepped out from his lodge. The wind was still blowing fiercely. *(whooshing of the wind)* He turned his face toward it and began his trek. He walked across the fields and through the woods. When he reached the foothills of the mountain, the wind began to blow even harder, and Gluscabi began to climb.

GLUSCABI: This wind will not beat me! I am Gluscabi, and I made myself! That should count for something.

NARRATOR: As Gluscabi made his way up the mountain, the wind blew so hard that it blew off his moccasins. *(Whoosh!)*

GLUSCABI: Who needs shoes? My feet are harder than any stone.

NARRATOR: Then the wind blew so hard that it blew off his shirt. *(Whoosh!)*

GLUSCABI: Who needs a shirt?

NARRATOR: Then the wind blew so hard that it blew off all his other clothes. *(Whoosh!)*

GLUSCABI: Oh well. I came into the world naked. I might as well be naked now.

NARRATOR: He had nearly reached the peak of the mountains, but then the greatest gust of wind blasted him. It was so powerful that it uprooted the hairs of his head. *(whooshing of wind, tearing of hair)* In an instant Glusacbi's hair and eyebrows were gone from his head.

GLUSCABI: *(cry of pain)* Argh!

NARRATOR: The wind knocked Gluscabi from his feet, and he clung desperately to a rocky crag.

GLUSCABI: *(yelling)* Hair—who needs it?

NARRATOR: For the first time he saw the great eagle. It was there on the mountain peak, beating its wings with all its might. Gluscabi felt his grip slipping, so he cried out to the supernatural beast.

GLUSCABI: *(yelling)* Grandfather! Stop! Let me speak to you!

NARRATOR: The eagle stopped beating its wings, and Gluscabi fell to the ground.

WUCHOWSEN: Who calls me grandfather?

GLUSCABI: *(panting)* I do! You about blew me off this mountain. I am Gluscabi.

WUCHOWSEN: Gluscabi? *(laugh)* What a stupid name! What does it mean?

GLUSCABI: It means "One who creates himself."

WUCHOWSEN: Really? I thought maybe it meant "goose droppings."

GLUSCABI: *(grumbling)*

WUCHOWSEN: You have a strange look about you. What happened to your hair?

GLUSCABI: You blew it off my head.

WUCHOWSEN: *(chuckles)* Yes, I know. There is no power like the wind. Now, why have you risked your life to come here?

GLUSCABI: To compliment you. You are just doing an excellent job with the wind these days.

WUCHOWSEN: Why thank you!

GLUSCABI: But as I climbed up here, I saw that mountain peak over there, and I thought, I bet the Great Eagle could make even more powerful wind from that peak.

WUCHOWSEN: More powerful wind, you say?

GLUSCABI: Of course! It is a much more scenic view from that peak, too.

WUCHOWSEN: Hmmm. I never thought of that. Thank you for the suggestion, hairless one. But how can I get from here to there?

GLUSCABI: Well, here's a thought—you could fly.

WUCHOWSEN: Hmmm. I will let you in on a little secret—I may have the most powerful wings in the world, but I am afraid to fly.

GLUSCABI: Then how did you get way up here?

WUCHOWSEN: I was born on this peak, and I plan to die on this peak.

GLUSCABI: Then I shall carry you myself.

WUCHOWSEN: Would you? How nice! I'm sorry I mocked you earlier.

GLUSCABI: Don't mention it. All I will need is a strap to help carry you.

NARRATOR: Gluscabi ran down the mountain until he came to a big basswood tree. He stripped off the outer bark, and from the inner bark he braided a strong strap. This he took back to the great eagle.

GLUSCABI: Let me wrap this around you to help me carry you.

NARRATOR: Gluscabi tied the strap around the eagle's body—cinching its wings down tightly to its sides. Then he lifted the eagle into the air.

GLUSCABI: I know just the perfect spot for you.

NARRATOR: He carried the eagle down the mountain a bit until he came to a deep crevice. Then he pitched the eagle down into the fissure.

WUCHOWSEN: Hey! What's going on? *(cry of shock)* Ahhhh!

NARRATOR: The bound eagle wedged in the crack—hanging upside down.

GLUSCABI: Ha! Who is goose droppings now, you old wind bag?

WUCHOWSEN: Come back here! You can't just leave me here!

GLUSCABI: Want to bet? Farewell!

NARRATOR: Gluscabi chuckled to himself as he walked back down the mountain—brushing his hands off with satisfaction.

GLUSCABI: I will have perfect duck-hunting weather now!

NARRATOR: But as he reached the foothills, he noticed how hot it was. There was no breeze to offset the heat of the sun. He at once got into his canoe and rowed out onto the bay.

GLUSCABI: Ugh. It is stifling.

NARRATOR: The air was so still and hot that it was hard to breathe. He noticed the water had grown foamy, turgid, and foul-smelling. He angrily rowed back to the shore and stalked into his lodge. Grandmother Woodchuck was by the doorway—sweat running down her fur.

WOODCHUCK: Gluscabi! Where are your clothes—and your hair?

GLUSCABI: Eh. I lost them.

WOODCHUCK: What did you do, Gluscabi? It's never been this still and miserable before. You didn't tamper with the wind eagle, did you?

GLUSCABI: He was messing up my duck hunt, so I messed *him* up!

WOODCHUCK: Won't you ever learn? Tabaldak, the Owner, set the wind eagle on that mountain peak for a reason. We need wind! The wind keeps the air cool and clean. The wind brings the clouds, which give us rain. The wind moves the waters.

GLUSCABI: Okay, okay. Kaamoji, Grandmother. I understand. *(pause)* Do I have to go fix things now?

WOODCHUCK: Yes! I'm sweating through my fur here!

NARRATOR: Gluscabi walked all the way back to the mountain peak, and he had never sweated so much in his life. When he reached the mountaintop, he could hear the feeble voice of the eagle calling out.

WUCHOWSEN: Hello? Is anyone there? I've fallen, and I can't get out.

NARRATOR: Gluscabi lowered his voice a bit and called out.

GLUSCABI: Who's there?

WUCHOWSEN: Oh, thank the Owner! It's me, the wind eagle. Some ugly, bald, naked man named Goose Droppings threw me down here.

GLUSCABI: I will get you out.

NARRATOR: Gluscabi drew the eagle out of the crevice—cutting the strap that bound its wings.

WUCHOWSEN: Ah, thank you—Hey! You're the one who put me down there!

GLUSCABI: Yes, and I apologize, grandfather. But let me tell you a bit of wisdom—it's good that the wind should blow sometimes, and other times it is good that it be still.

NARRATOR: The eagle thought for a moment.

WUCHOWSEN: Grandson, I hear what you say.

GLUSCABI: Thank you.

NARRATOR: Gluscabi helped the wind eagle return to its perch. To this day sometimes there is wind, and sometimes it is still. When Gluscabi reached his lodge, Grandmother Woodchuck was waiting for him.

GLUSCABI: I think I have learned my lesson, Grandmother—not to interfere with nature.

WOODCHUCK: You have learned not to use your powers for evil, but you must also learn how to use them for good.

NARRATOR: Near where Gluscabi and Grandmother Woodchuck lived, there was a village of humans. Every day Gluscabi watched them with great curiosity because they were so much like him—but so much different. They grew their crops, raised their families, and lived their lives. But one day the river that they used for their livelihood dried up, and they at once became alarmed.

MAN: The water! Where has it gone?

CHIEF: Someone must go upriver and see what is causing the river to stop flowing!

NARRATOR: One man volunteered, and he returned with a terrifying story.

MAN: There is a dam built across the river—holding back the water. And there are hideous monsters guarding it—monsters ten feet tall with long, deadly fingers.

CHIEF: What did they say when you asked for our water to be returned?

MAN: They threw this at me.

NARRATOR: It was a wooden cup filled with mud.

MAN: They said this is all we shall have.

CHIEF: We will just see about that! Warriors, prepare your spears and bows! We will defeat these monsters.

(shouting of warriors)

NARRATOR: The war band embarked, full of the hope of glory, but only a single warrior returned—his body bloody and broken.

WARRIOR: *(weakly)* The monsters—they crushed our warriors in their grip. They slung them about like helpless animals and broke them upon the ground. And I saw their chief monster. He is the worst of them all. He is even bigger than the rest—with huge, bulging eyes and a mouth that could swallow the sun.

CHIEF: Then all is lost! No one alive could ever defeat such a monster.

NARRATOR: Gluscabi, who happened to be watching all of this from the wood, stepped forward.

GLUSCABI: I can defeat this monster!

CHIEF: Who are you?

GLUSCABI: I am the one called Gluscabi. Perhaps you have heard of me?

NARRATOR: The chief drew back in fright.

GLUSCABI: Don't worry. I am not causing mischief this time. I am going to use my powers for good. I will go and defeat this monster for you.

NARRATOR: Gluscabi painted his face half white and half black—preparing for battle. Then he walked up the dry river bed. In its path lay many dead animals, fish of all kinds and turtles.

GLUSCABI: This monster is hoarding all the water for himself, and that is wrong. I have learned this lesson before, and I am happy to teach it to him.

NARRATOR: He stopped along the way and fashioned a mighty club from the trunk of a tree. Then he walked on. At last he reached the massive dam. Standing upon it were menacing-looking monsters with green, warty skin and long, thin arms.

GUARD: Grawk! Who dares approach the dam?

GLUSCABI: Gluscabi does.

GUARD: Goose droppings? *(loud laughter)*

GLUSCABI: The only dropping you will see is the sight of your comrades dropping to the ground.

GUARD: *(angrily)* Kill him!

NARRATOR: The monsters pounced down upon Gluscabi, but he was too quick for them. *(shrieking of monsters)* Using his mighty club, he smashed their bones and sent them flying in all directions. *(sounds of a fight)* Soon all the monsters lay in a motionless heap upon the ground.

GLUSCABI: Now give me some water.

NARRATOR: A deep, guttural roar boomed over the top of the dam.

MONSTER: *(roaring deeply)* Give him none! Give him none!

GLUSCABI: Show yourself, you greedy monster! Or are you going to hide behind your dam forever?

NARRATOR: There was no response.

GLUSCABI: I will take that as a "yes."

NARRATOR: Gluscabi knew he could not break the dam by himself, so he turned his face toward the tall mountain peak.

GLUSCABI: Grandfather Wuchowsen, I know I do not deserve your help, but I seek it now. Show me the power of the wind once again.

NARRATOR: Faraway, Gluscabi heard the screech of an eagle. *(eagle screech)* A mighty wind began to blow against the monsters' dam, and Gluscabi smote it with his massive club. *(crashing sound)* The dam broke, and the water came rushing forth. Gluscabi jumped to the side, and the lifeless bodies of the monsters were washed downstream. *(rushing water)*

GLUSCABI: Now, once again, the waters are free—as they should be.

NARRATOR: Two demonic, yellow eyes rose above the surface of the river, and a horrible croaking filled the air.

MONSTER: Roark! Roark! How dare you, miserable human!

GLUSCABI: I am not a human. I am Gluscabi.

MONSTER: I do not care what you are! I will devour you!

NARRATOR: The monster rose from the water, opening his enormous mouth—intent on swallowing Gluscabi whole. And, in fact, that is exactly what he did. Gluscabi disappeared down the monster's massive maw.

MONSTER: *(gulp)* Mmmmm.

NARRATOR: But Gluscabi did not stay there long. The belly of the monster began to rumble. *(rumbling sound)* And then the monster let out a horrible choking sound.

MONSTER: *(choking and coughing)*

NARRATOR: The monster's long tongue shot out, and Gluscabi rode upon the end of it—his club at the ready. He jumped high into the air and brought the club down hard upon the monster's warty head. *(Shazam!)* The monster rolled back into the water—gasping for breath.

MONSTER: How? How can you defeat me? No creature made by the Owner can defeat me!

GLUSCABI: Then you have answered your own question. I made myself.

NARRATOR: It was either that Gluscabi grew bigger or the monster grew smaller, but soon the monster was small enough for Gluscabi to reach out and grab in his hand. Gluscabi lifted him up and looked him straight in his round, yellow eyes.

GLUSCABI: So you like to squeeze the life out of others, huh?

NARRATOR: He squeezed the monster, and its eyes bugged out of its head even more. *(squeaking sound)*

GLUSCABI: You greedy little toad. I will spare your miserable life, but from now on you will be nothing but a bullfrog.

NARRATOR: Then Gluscabi tossed the frog back into the roaring river. To this day you can still hear the bullfrog trying to claim what he cannot own—forever croaking, "Give him none. Give him none."

Gluscabi returned to the human village. The chief was overjoyed when he saw him.

CHIEF: The water has returned! When we saw the water flowing again, some of my people were so overjoyed that they jumped in and became fish and river creatures themselves.

GLUSCABI: They must help protect these waters. No one can ever own them. They must be shared with everyone.

36   Searching for America

NARRATOR: When Gluscabi returned to his lodge, Grandmother Woodchuck was waiting for him.

GLUSCABI: Well, Grandmother. Have I finally learned my lesson?

WOODCHUCK: Gluscabi, I am so proud of you!

GLUSCABI: Oleohneh, Grandmother.

NARRATOR: So Gluscabi became a great teacher for the humans—helping them see that the earth is not their own. It is a force that should not be tampered with and a treasure to be shared with all that live and breathe. It was a lesson that he had learned first and was happy to share with others.

DISCUSSION QUESTIONS

1. What is interesting about the way in which Gluscabi comes into existence?
2. What lesson does Gluscabi learn in his adventure with the magical game bag?
3. What lesson does Gluscabi learn in his adventure with the wind eagle?
4. What lesson does Gluscabi learn in his adventure with the dammed river?
5. What details about nature do the myths of Gluscabi explain?
6. In many Native American cultures animals are not treated as inferior to humans but rather as brothers and sisters. How is this reflected in Gluscabi's stories?

EXPLORERS OF THE NEW WORLD
TEACHER GUIDE

BACKGROUND

Getting rich quick has always been a part of the lure of America—whether we Americans would like to admit it or not. While settlers came to the New World for religious freedom or liberty from other persecution, many others came seeking wealth. Some of the first European explorers to arrive in America expected to find untold treasures, cities of gold, and even the fountain of youth. Needless to say, in this, they were disappointed.

What they *did* find was a land rich with natural resources—and a population of natives that they viewed as part of those resources—both upon which they were quick to capitalize. Horrible atrocities were committed against the natives. Some explorers forced them into slavery. Others just wiped them out to make way for their own conquests. It was a rare case when the explorers developed an appreciation of the natives as fellow human beings. In the end it was not gold that made the explorers rich, but their ability to exploit what they found here.

While this ignoble time in America's history was filled with cruelty and greed, it serves as an important lesson. America is a land of opportunity, a place where even the lowly can find success; however, if that success comes at the expense of others, it is a success not worth having. It is a lesson that our country had to learn along the way.

As you read about the various groups of people who first came to America, think about their motivations. Many of their reasons for seeking America are the same reasons immigrants come to America today.

SUMMARY

One by one, the first European explorers of North America explain their role in the exploration and settlement of America. Christopher Columbus describes how he received financing from the King and Queen of Spain in order to sail across the Atlantic to search for a passage to the East Indies. When he accidentally arrived on a new continent, he believed he had reached India and named the natives there *Indians*. Amerigo Vespucci, an Italian explorer, explains how he helped clear up this misconception by convincing the Europeans that they had discovered a new continent. Because of his role, America is named after him. Leif Ericson, the Viking explorer, interjects, telling how the Vikings actually arrived in America 500 years before Columbus. When the natives attacked the Viking explorers, they were forced to leave.

Like many of the first explorers, the Spanish hoped to find gold and treasure in the New World. Next, Cabeza de Vaca, a Spanish Conquistador, describes his journey across Texas and his capture by the Indians there. Unlike Columbus, who viewed the Indians as complete savages, Cabeza de Vaca came to appreciate their culture before he managed to escape.

British explorer Sir Walter Raleigh is the next to describe his role in the New World. He was commissioned by Elizabeth I to establish the first English colony in America, Roanoke Colony. After thriving for many years, the colonists at Roanoke mysteriously disappeared leaving only the words *Croatoan* and *Cro* carved into landmarks near the settlement. Raleigh also tells of Virginia Dare, the first English child to be born in America. According to legend, she was transformed into a white deer.

John Smith, an adventurer commissioned

by James I to make a new settlement called Jamestown in the New World, tells of his interactions with the Indian chief Powhatan and the chief's daughter, Pocahontas. When Smith was about to be executed by Powhatan, Pocahontas threw her body over his, saving his life.

Powhatan and Pocahontas both speak, and Pocahontas tells of her journey to Europe, where she fell sick and died. Although the first explorers were often inhumane in their treatment of the Native Americans, their sense of adventure and desire for success influenced the spirit of America.

ESSENTIAL QUESTIONS

- What motivated the first European explorers of America?
- How was America shaped by these first explorers?

CONNECT

The General History of Virginia by **John Smith** Captain John's Smith narrative about his exploits in the New World made the famous explorer a bestselling author. Some have questioned how much actual fact found its way into his writing. In particular, his colorful dramatic rescue by Pocahontas has been challenged as a romantic embellishment.

ANTICIPATORY QUESTIONS

- Who were some of the first European explorers to come to North America?
- What were some of the reasons explorers came to America?
- If you thought you could obtain great wealth, would you travel to a new world? Explain.
- What do you know about the story of Pocahontas?

TEACHABLE TERMS

- **Alliteration** On pg. 41 when Columbus claims the other explorers were "feebly following in my footsteps," this is a use of alliteration.
- **Puns** Examples of punny wordplay are on pg. 41 when Columbus asks Leif Ericson if he had to *Leif* instead of *leave* and on pg. 42 when Vespucci makes a variety of cow puns on the meaning of Cabeza de Vaca's name.
- **Tone** Although the details mentioned in this script-story are accurate, the author presents them with a humorous tone, poking fun at the featured explorers.
- **Characterization** Analyze the explorers' motivations for wanting to explore the New World. Did they all have similar motivations?

RECALL QUESTIONS

1. Why did Christopher Columbus name the Native Americans *Indians*?
2. What group of explorers visited America 500 years before the other European explorers?
3. What did most of the explorers hope to find in the New World?
4. What was the only clue left behind after the settlers of Roanoke Colony vanished?
5. According to legend, how did Pocahontas save the life of John Smith?

THE EXPLORERS OF THE NEW WORLD

CAST

COLUMBUS	*Famed Explorer*
VESPUCCI	*Italian Explorer*
POLO	*Italian Explorer*
ERICSON	*Viking Explorer*
DE VACA	*Spanish Conquistador*
RALEIGH	*English Explorer*
SMITH	*English Adventurer*
POCAHONTAS	*Indian Princess*
POWHATAN	*Indian Chief*

(A series of European explorers and two Native Americans sit upon a blank stage. A banner that reads, "Welcome, Explorers," hangs overhead.)

POLO: Greetings, young people! I will be your host for this evening. I am the explorer who first discovered a trade route from Europe to the exotic lands of Asia. My name is Marco…

ALL: *(screaming)* Polo!

POLO: *(looking shocked)* Yes. I guess you have heard of me. As our special guests tonight are some of history's greatest explorers. We had to alter the space-time continuum a bit to gather them all together, but it will be worth it. What could go wrong?

We asked students from across the globe to send in letters asking these explorers important questions. Once we explained to them what a letter was, we got many responses. Here is the first one. *(reading)* "Dear explorers, who first discovered America?"

COLUMBUS: I'll answer that question because the answer is simple—*me*! I am Christopher Columbus, famed explorer, and *I* discovered America!

VESPUCCI: *(clearing his throat)* I think not! *I* discovered America!

COLUMBUS: Wanna bet? In 1492 *Columbus* sailed the ocean blue—not whatever your name is.

VESPUCCI: I am Amerigo Vespucci, and as you notice, America is named after me.

COLUMBUS: Ignore this ignorant Italian!

VESPUCCI: I thought you were an Italian as well.

COLUMBUS: Well, it is debatable. Some historians—who have nothing better to do—have argued that I might be Portuguese. As I was saying…growing up, I wanted to be an explorer just like my hero, Marco—

ALL: *(screaming)* Polo!

COLUMBUS: In his travels he had explored Asia and had grown rich in the process. Why wouldn't I want to follow in his footsteps?

POLO: Naturally.

COLUMBUS: But while Marco…

ALL: *(screaming)* Polo!

COLUMBUS: Had sailed all the way around Africa, I thought I could find a new route to the East Indies by sailing west.

VESPUCCI: Sailing west to get east. That was your big idea? How brilliant.

COLUMBUS: It was a brilliant idea, but I needed someone to finance my voyage. After being rejected by the King of Portugal—

VESPUCCI: Not to mention most of the women of that country…

COLUMBUS: I made my way to Spain, where Queen Isabella and King Ferdinand granted my request for three ships—the Niña, the Pinta, and the Santa Maria. And I did it all before this Vespucci fool!

VESPUCCI: I have always wondered—if your people are called the Portuguese, is just one of you called a Portugoose?

COLUMBUS: *You're* the goose! Anyway, picture it! I had my ships! Bravely I sailed across the ocean—never knowing what I would find.

VESPUCCI: I heard that you still thought the world was flat!

COLUMBUS: Ha! Any fool knows that the world is round.

VESPUCCI: Any fool, huh? Then I guess you *do* know it.

POLO: Gentlemen, please.

(Extremely irritated, Columbus straightens his doublet.)

COLUMBUS: I sailed westward, but the path to Asia was blocked by a new land I had not anticipated.

VESPUCCI: There's not much that's heroic about sailing across the sea and accidentally bumping into something that you didn't know was there.

COLUMBUS: Yeah, but I bumped into it first, and that counts for something! Because of this, I am the first American hero!

VESPUCCI: Yet it is named after *me*! Explain that one, Mr. Hero. You never made it to *North* America. You ran ashore on the islands of the Bahamas.

COLUMBUS: America's capital is named after me—the District of Columbia.

VESPUCCI: How impressive. Not.

COLUMBUS: I discovered the New World!

VESPUCCI: But you were too dumb to realize it. You kept insisting it was the East Indies. You even called the natives there *Indians*.

COLUMBUS: How was I supposed to know where I was?

VESPUCCI: It wasn't until my voyages years later that I convinced people that we Europeans had, in fact, discovered a new world.

COLUMBUS: Meanwhile, while you were feebly following in my footsteps, the Spanish king had made *me* the governor of the new land I had discovered.

VESPUCCI: Oh yes. And what a good governor you were! You captured the natives and sold them off as slaves. How noble of you!

(Leif Ericson, a hulking Viking man, steps between Columbus and Vespucci.)

ERICSON: Argh! I can't take this anymore! You're both wrong! *I* was the first person to discover the New World.

COLUMBUS: Who are you? And what is that horrible smell?

ERICSON: It is my Viking manliness! A combination of mead-breath and body odor! *(sniffs armpit)* I am Leif Ericson! My Viking ancestors and I visited the New World 500 years before any of the rest of you so-called explorers did.

COLUMBUS: Then why, pray tell, did you not stay?

ERICSON: We would have, but we ran into some of the natives, and those little boogers were fierce fighters!

COLUMBUS: So, you ran? Ha! Things got tough, so you had to *Leif.* Ha!

ERICSON: Is that a pun? No one makes a pun on my name. Argh!

(Leif Ericson raises up an enormous axe and chases Christopher Columbus off the stage.)

COLUMBUS: *(cry of fright)* Ah!

POLO: Well, we have heard from the Portuguese, Italian, and Nordic explorers. What about the Spanish? Next we have Cabeza de Vaca.

(Cabeza de Vaca, dressed like a conquistador, steps forward.)

DE VACA: Hola, niños. While the other foolish Europeans were arguing about who made it to the New World first, we Spanish were busy searching for treasure there.

RALEIGH: Ha! That is just like the Spanish! Always gold-digging!

DE VACA: And just what were *you* doing in the New World?

RALEIGH: *(sheepishly)* Looking for gold.

DE VACA: That's what I thought. My adventures brought honor to the name of Cabeza de Vaca.

VESPUCCI: Doesn't your name mean "head of a cow"?

DE VACA: It does. Do you have a problem with that?

VESPUCCI: No, but *you* should.

DE VACA: In 1528 I landed with 400 soldiers to explore the western coast of Florida. Seven years earlier, my fellow conquistador, Ponce de Leon, had explored Florida—reportedly searching for the Fountain of Youth.

POLO: Did he find it?

DE VACA: He is dead and so am I. What do you think? *(pause)* While in Florida, my troops and I ran out of provisions, and we were forced to sail to Mexico in five flimsy boats. Most of the men drowned. Then we reached a place more hostile than all the rest—Texas.

VESPUCCI: Oooh. Sounds frightening.

DE VACA: It was! After a horrible winter in Texas, only four of us were alive. Then we were captured by the Indians and spent the next several years as captives.

VESPUCCI: I bet that was a humbling experience for you—even more humiliating than being named "cow head."

DE VACA: Grrr. I learned to appreciate the native people on a whole new level. I even assimilated into their culture a bit. I even became a great healer among them! *(shouting)* Be healed! They revered me as a medicine man.

VESPUCCI: In other words you really *cowed* them with your *bull*.

DE VACA: Once I was trusted by their culture, I managed to escape and fled all the way to Mexico City.

VESPUCCI: Wow. I bet you really had to *hoof* it.

DE VACA: That's it! No more cow jokes!

VESPUCCI: Don't have a cow, man.

DE VACA: I do not have to stand here and be insulted like this!

VESPUCCI: Then sit down—and let someone else talk for a change.

(Cabeza de Vaca storms off the stage.)

VESPUCCI: Stampede! The herd's on the move!

POLO: *(sigh)* Next we have an English explorer, the revered Sir Walter Really.

RALEIGH: It's pronounced *Raleigh*.

POLO: Raleigh? Really? Okay. Sir Walter Raleigh.

(Sir Walter Raleigh steps forward. He is wearing an oversized, frilly collar and laughably poofy pants.)

POLO: Also with him is famed English adventurer, John Smith.

(John Smith, a simply-dressed man with a musket, steps forward.)

RALEIGH: Greetings. I am the famed English explorer, Sir Walter Raleigh. I helped organize the first English colony in America.

SMITH: And I am famed adventurer, John Smith. I, too, was—

RALEIGH: *(interrupting)* I'll take it from here, Smith. If I need your opinion, I'll beat it out of you. We English came a bit late to the New World. I had led my own expeditions to South America searching for a legendary city of gold called El Dorado.

SMITH: *(sarcastically)* Tell them how that worked out for you.

RALEIGH: Unfortunately, I did not find it, but my men and I did make several important discoveries.

SMITH: Like new exotic types of diarrhea.

RALEIGH: Silence, Smith! But since I had such excellent exploring expertise, my queen, her highness, Elizabeth I, the Virgin Queen of England, held me in high regard.

SMITH: I heard she held you quite a bit!

RALEIGH: Ha! My relationship with Her Majesty was completely innocent. She commissioned me to organize the first English colony in the New World in a region we named "Virginia" after her.

SMITH: What a brown-noser! Sir Raleigh, if you were so brave, why did you send common men like me to set up your colonies for you?

RALEIGH: I couldn't go myself! I was far too busy!

SMITH: Doing what? Flirting with the queen?

RALEIGH: Talk to the hand, Smith.

SMITH: Really, Raleigh? Is that the best you can do?

RALEIGH: The first English colony in the New World was on Roanoke Island. The colony thrived for many years, and it was home to the first English colonist born in the New World—a little girl named Virginia Dare. She would become the stuff of legend.

SMITH: I think those pants you are wearing are the stuff of legend. For rich lords like Sir Raleigh the point of the colonies was to make quick, easy money. For the rest of us, we just wanted to make a fresh start for ourselves in the New World.

RALEIGH: You should start with a fresh set of clothes. You reek! In spite of my expert planning, Roanoke Colony was doomed to be short lived. When the leader of the colony sailed back to England for supplies, he could not return for three years because war broke out with the Spanish. Those cursed Spanish! I spit when I say their name! Ptoo! Ptoo!

SMITH: *(wiping spit off him)* Watch it.

RALEIGH: When he finally returned to Roanoke, the colonists had disappeared! The houses had been dismantled in a seemingly orderly way. The only clue was the word *Croatoan* carved into a post of the fort and *Cro* on a nearby tree.

VESPUCCI: Maybe they were eaten by a large crow.

RALEIGH: That is just stupid.

VESPUCCI: So is searching for a city made out of gold.

RALEIGH: Touché.

SMITH: There was an island nearby named Croatoan, and the Indians who lived there used that name for their tribe. So it was assumed that perhaps the Indians had killed or abducted the colonists. But if the colonists had run into trouble, they were expected to carve a cross into a tree. No such symbol was found.

VESPUCCI: Maybe the giant crow ate them all before they could carve a cross.

SMITH: All I know is if I had been there, the people would have been safe! *(shakes musket)*

POLO: But no one knows if Indians were to blame. The colonists could have tried to sail back to England or joined up with the Indians to survive. They could have also been massacred by the Spanish.

RALEIGH: That's the most believable option. Those filthy Spaniards! Ptoo! Ptoo!

SMITH: *(wiping spit off himself again)* All kinds of legends exist about the Lost Colony of Roanoke and the first English-American child, Virginia Dare. There was a story of an all-white doe that was shot by a hunter. When the hunter drew near to it, the doe spoke to him and said the name "Virginia Dare."

VESPUCCI: See? If Virginia Dare was magically transformed into a deer, my man-eating crow theory is looking better all the time!

SMITH: Since Roanoke the Lost Colony was such a failure, the next time England sent over a batch of colonists, they appointed *me* to go with them. I was born poor…

RALEIGH: Obviously. *(snicker)*

SMITH: And unlike Lord Bouncy-Britches here, I *earned* my fame. He just got his from being a lord and flirting with the queen.

RALEIGH: It worked, didn't it?

SMITH: A little too well. Sir Raleigh finally got what was coming to him. When he dared get married to another woman without the queen's permission, she locked him up in the Tower of London and planned to have him executed.

RALEIGH: *(sigh)* She did it out of love though.

VESPUCCI: What did she see in him? Must be the pants.

SMITH: Or desperation. She *had* been single for forty years. *(pause)* Before I traveled to the New World, I had become famous for my adventures all over the world. The new king, James I, thought I would be just what the next batch of colonists needed to survive in the New World—and he was right! I accompanied the Virginia Company over to America and helped them set up a new colony named Jamestown after the king.

RALEIGH: Who is the brown-noser now?

SMITH: What made it so rough is that the men in charge were a bunch of noble stuffed-shirts similar to Sir Raleigh here. They didn't believe they needed to work like the other men.

RALEIGH: Ha! Work? I would get my tights dirty!

SMITH: Because of their leadership, we about starved! They were busy looking for gold when they should have been trying to grow crops. Since we had arrived, we had seen natives in the forest. They were the people of the mighty chief Powhatan and his allies.

POLO: Tonight we have Chief Powhatan and his daughter, Pocahontas, with us.

(Powhatan, wearing ceremonial garments, and his daughter, Pocahontas, step forward.)

POWHATAN: When I heard that the white man had landed on our shores, it filled me with fear. I summoned all my war leaders to see what must be done. We decided not to give our aid to the white man.

POCAHONTAS: Don't forget about my part of the story, Father.

POWHATAN: Of course not, daughter. Pocahontas is not my daughter's real name. It is a nickname that means "naughty one," and it fits her well. She was always sneaking off to spy on the English white men as they struggled to build their fort and scratch a living out of the unforgiving ground.

POCAHONTAS: At first my father tried to do everything he could to starve the white men out, but I went to their fort and took them food behind his back.

POWHATAN: I slowly realized that the white man was not going anywhere. I was an ambitious leader, and I saw the white man had great power. So I made him my ally.

SMITH: When I was out hunting in the woods once, I was captured by the Indians, and they took me back to Powhatan's camp. I thought I would be killed for sure. They tied my hands behind my back and forced my head down upon a rock. Powhatan himself raised his club over me—ready to smash out my brains. But then Pocahontas ran forward and laid her head over mine—shielding me—saving me from death. After that I was adopted into their tribe.

RALEIGH: *(scoffing)* Ha! What a story! Imagine a bloodthirsty savage giving her life for a white man.

SMITH: Well, it may have been an Indian ceremony that I didn't understand.

POCAHONTAS: It is a scene that has been romanticized for many years.

VESPUCCI: Romance? Weren't you eleven, and he was nearly thirty?

POCAHONTAS: We were not in love, but we were great friends. Although I might have had a girlish crush on him!

RALEIGH: If I had been there, she would have been totally head over heels!

SMITH: So the Indians became our allies. Since we had nearly starved and I seemed to be the only one with common sense, the colonists of Jamestown put me in charge. I made a new rule—if you do not work, you do not eat.

RALEIGH: Ludicrous! Some of us are just born supervisors.

SMITH: I sent some of my men to live in Powhatan's tribe to learn his language and culture. Once when I was speaking to Powhatan, I mentioned the Lost Colony of Roanoke. He claimed that it was his people that had gone to the island and wiped out the settlers there. But I never knew if this was the truth or a misunderstanding between us.

POCAHONTAS: As for me, everything about the English fascinated me. I began to wonder what their land was like.

SMITH: Although I helped Jamestown survive in the New World, I was not popular among the people of the colony. Some of the colonists were plotting my murder, but Pocahontas warned me, and I was able to avoid such a fate. But sometime afterward I was injured in a gun powder explosion, and I was forced to return to England for medical treatment.

RALEIGH: Not as tough as you thought, were you?

SMITH: Once I healed, I became a bestselling author! Everyone in England was eager to read of my adventures.

POCAHONTAS: Back in the New World, I heard a rumor that my friend John Smith had died. I was heartbroken.

POWHATAN: Jamestown continued to thrive because the English modified one of our crops—tobacco—and began to ship it over to Europe. It made the white man wealthy.

POCAHONTAS: It also brought a man named John Rolfe to the colony. I met him there, and I became his wife. Then he took me back to England with him. I met royalty and lived the life of a celebrity. While I was in England, I learned that my old friend, John Smith, was actually alive.

RALEIGH: Awkward…

POCAHONTAS: When I saw that he was actually alive, I would not even speak to him. Soon after, I died mysteriously. Some say I contracted a sickness. Others say I was poisoned. I was only twenty-one.

RALEIGH: *(sigh)* I died, too. I offended King James, and he had me executed.

SMITH: You couldn't flirt your way out of that one, could you?

RALEIGH: No. And I lost my head. Literally. We all eventually went the way of the grave. But our names live on as the first discoverers and explorers of America.

POWHATAN: But remember—my people had been here hundreds of years, maybe thousands of years, before you white men arrived. No man can claim to be the true discoverer of America.

SMITH: Wisely spoken, chief. What we *did* discover in the New World was a new spirit. It was a land full of adventure!

RALEIGH: And surprisingly empty of gold.

POCAHONTAS: What America had was better than gold. It had opportunity!

VESPUCCI: And an extremely catchy name!

POCAHONTAS: The same spirit that led these explorers leads us on today—to better and brighter things.

POWHATAN: What worlds will we explore next? What new chapters await our country? Only time will tell.

POLO: This program tonight is a message to all of you Americans sitting in your comfy seats enjoying the freedoms of the New World, which now seems so old! *(pointing to the audience)* Yes, I mean you. These intrepid men and women who explored the new continent deserve your praise!

VESPUCCI: Even the one named after a cow's head.

(The audience stands and claps for the explorers.)

POLO: So, search on, you new explorers! I am your host, Marco—

ALL: *(screaming)* Polo!

POLO: *(sigh)* I really hate that. Continue discovering the spirit of America. Thank you and good night!

DISCUSSION QUESTIONS

1. Compare and contrast some of the different reasons explorers came to the New World. How did they have different motivations?
2. Christopher Columbus is often celebrated as a hero. Does he deserve this status?
3. What do you think happened to the Lost Colony? Explain.
4. What made John Smith different from many of the other explorers?
5. Was Pocahontas a hero? Explain.
6. Are there any "new worlds" left to explore today? Explain.

MAYFLOWER
TEACHER GUIDE

BACKGROUND

Religious freedom is one of the rights guaranteed to every American citizen by the Constitution of the United States. The seeds of this right were laid long before the drafters of the Constitution were ever born. Many of the first immigrants to North America understood that religions controlled by governments were severely flawed—knowledge they gained from personal experience. The group of religious immigrants we call the Pilgrims were no exception.

The Pilgrims' story is one of faith and courage that still resonates deeply today. William Bradford, whose journal *Of Plymouth Plantation* forms the basis for this script-story, was the Pilgrims' greatest leader. His firsthand account of their voyage highlights the great personal conviction it took for such a courageous undertaking. Without the heroism of these Pilgrims, America might not be the place it is today—a place where all are free to worship as they choose.

SUMMARY

Separatists are a group of objectors in 1600's England who seek to separate from the Church of England. They feel that the state-run church, headed by King James I, has violated the principles of true Christianity. These reformers eventually earn the named *Puritans* for their attempts to "purify" the church. The king persecutes them for their beliefs, mutilating some and throwing others into prison. To escape this persecution, a group of Separatists called Pilgrims decide to pool their money together and sail to Holland, a land known for religious tolerance. Young William Bradford, going against the wishes of his family, accompanies these Pilgrims as they set out for Holland.

Life in Holland does not prove to be as wholesome as the Puritans hoped, so they set their sights on the New World and obtain permission to sail to the Jamestown settlement in North America. When problems with their ship, the *Speedwell*, force them to abort their first voyage, the Pilgrims set out in another ship, the *Mayflower*.

It takes the Pilgrims sixty-six days of sailing to reach the New World. During this time many of the Pilgrims suffer from malnutrition and scurvy. One Pilgrim woman gives birth to a son, Oceanus, in the midst of their voyage. The Pilgrims' strained finances have forced them to share the voyage with other passengers, who are not Separatists, and these passengers often mock the Pilgrims for their faith.

Once upon the voyage, the main beam of the *Mayflower* cracks, but one Pilgrim has brought along a screw jack and is able to repair this beam. During a storm, one man is lost overboard but is saved when he manages to grab ahold of a rope. Only one Pilgrim, a young boy, dies on the voyage to the New World.

Whenever the Pilgrims reach the New World, they realize that they are far off course and have missed Jamestown completely. Aboard the *Mayflower* the Pilgrims and the other passengers draft the *Mayflower Compact*, a document of self-governance, which is the first of its kind in America. While Bradford and other leaders leave the ship to scout out the mainland, Bradford's wife falls from the *Mayflower* and drowns. It is unclear whether she fell or jumped intentionally.

Now the settlers are faced with the prospect of building shelter for themselves in a hostile wilderness. It is during this time half of the Pilgrims take sick and die from the wintery conditions.

When spring comes, representatives from the local Indian tribe arrive to greet the Pilgrims peacefully. An Indian named Squanto, who has lived in Europe as a slave, shows the Pilgrims how to plant Indian corn. The Pilgrims and the Indians make a treaty between themselves. To celebrate their survival through the brutal winter, the Pilgrims hold a celebratory feast, which becomes known as the first Thanksgiving.

ESSENTIAL QUESTIONS

- Why is religious freedom important?
- How much are you willing to sacrifice for what you believe?

CONNECT

The Mayflower Compact (1620) On pg. 55 the Pilgrims create a document, along with their non-Pilgrim companions, called *The Mayflower Compact*. Historians have noted that this document signed aboard the *Mayflower* is America's first document of self-government. The signers agreed to abide by the laws set forth by the document. This was important first step toward a democratic American government. Read a copy of this document and analyze it to see if you can spot the first hints of American democracy within it.

ANTICIPATORY QUESTIONS

- Who were the Pilgrims?
- How do you celebrate Thanksgiving?
- Would you be willing to risk your life for religious freedom?

TEACHABLE TERMS

- **Personal Narrative** William Bradford's *Of Plymouth Plantation* is one of the earliest examples of an American personal narrative, a prose account of a person's life experiences usually told in first person.
- **Theme: The Providence of God** Throughout the story of the Pilgrims' voyage, Bradford frequently alludes to the Providence of God and His intervention in their journey. An example of this is found on pg. 54 when Bradford tells how a young man was kept from drowning. On pg. 56 Bradford also credits God for keeping some of the Pilgrims from sickness. On pg. 59 Bradford says he sees the hand of God in every instance of their voyage.
- **Situational Irony** Although the Pilgrims expected the Indians to be hostile, when the Indians do finally come to their settlement on pg. 57, they come in peace.
- **Important Term:** *Puritan* The Pilgrims' journey was born out of the Puritan reformation in England. Although many Puritans chose to remain in England, the Pilgrims were Puritans who made a choice to leave England. The term *Puritan* was later applied to the descendants of the Pilgrims in America.

RECALL QUESTIONS

1. Why did the Pilgrims want to leave England?
2. To which country did the Pilgrims journey before coming to America?
3. What is the *Mayflower Compact*?
4. How did William Bradford's wife die?
5. How did Squanto assist the Pilgrims?

MAYFLOWER:
THE VOYAGE OF THE PILGRIMS

ADAPTED FROM THE JOURNAL OF WILLIAM BRADFORD

NARRATOR ONE	*Teller of the Tale*
NARRATOR TWO	*Teller of the Tale*
BRADFORD	*Leader of the Pilgrims*
PREACHER	*Separatist Preacher*
KING JAMES	*Ruler of England*
CAPTAIN	*Captain of the Ship*
SAILOR	*Cruel Sailor*
HOWLAND	*Young Pilgrim*
STANDISH	*Military Commander*
STRANGER	*Passenger on the Ship*
SAMOSET	*Native American*
SQUANTO	*Native American*

NARRATOR ONE: On Thanksgiving there is no scene more familiar than a table filled with Pilgrims and Native American Indians sharing a celebratory feast. But behind this simple scene there is a story to tell—a story that reminds us why faith and freedom are two of our nation's greatest legacies.

NARRATOR TWO: Our story begins in England—in the 1600's—with a group of devout Christians called the Separatists and a young man named William Bradford.

BRADFORD: When I was just twelve years old, I was sitting in a church meeting in my village of Austerfield—listening to the minister mumble some verses from his prayer-book. As I listened to his speech, I felt nothing. No connection to God. No divine spirit. I knew something was missing.

NARRATOR ONE: Young Bradford was not alone in these convictions. A group of church-reformers called the Puritans felt that the Church of England had grown corrupt. They were called "Puritans" because they wanted the church to return to the purity of early Christianity—leaving behind many of the rituals they had acquired from years of tradition.

BRADFORD: I remember that upon my town's stone church there was a carving of a serpent. I felt that the Church of England had been poisoned by the venom of that old snake, Satan, and something must be done about it.

NARRATOR TWO: With this conviction burning in his heart, William learned that a group of Puritans met in a secret location in Scrooby, a town a few miles down the road. These men had to meet in secret because they were a branch of the Puritans called Separatists—which meant they wanted to separate from the Church of England.

BRADFORD: Oh, King James! He did not want us Separatists to challenge his church—

the *only* church available in England. Many Separatists had been imprisoned and died in jail. But I went to seek them out all the same. I knew that God was calling me.

PREACHER: This cannot continue! It is time we break free from the Church of England once and for all! Was it for this that Christ died? Meaningless rituals? Stale theology? There has to be more than this! The Church of England is corrupt beyond all hope!

BRADFORD: I began to meet regularly with the Separatists. When my family found out I had been going to these church meetings, they forbade me to go back—but still I went. Then conditions in England—even though already unfriendly toward Separatists—grew worse.

KING JAMES: *(angrily)* How dare they defy me! I will harry these Separatists out of England—by any means I can!

BRADFORD: As the persecution increased, we reminded ourselves that we were just pilgrims—travelers—in this cruel world. We remembered that heaven above was our true home, and this quieted our spirits.

NARRATOR TWO: The persecutions by King James grew worse. Separatists were thrown in jail. Some of them had their noses split and their ears lopped off. Some were executed. It would have been simple for these good people to continue about their daily business and not risk their lives for their faith, but they felt called to something more.

NARRATOR ONE: Finally, many of the Separatists knew they must do the unthinkable—leave behind the place they had always called home. They must go where they could worship God freely. But where did such a place exist?

PREACHER: Brothers, Holland may be our only hope. It is known throughout Europe for its tolerance. People of all religious faiths find sanctuary there.

NARRATOR ONE: And so the Separatists became Pilgrims—men and women on a holy journey. They pooled their money, secretly chartered a ship, and boarded with their families—thinking they would find a new home in Holland.

BRADFORD: I was just seventeen when I made the decision to flee with my group to Holland. On our first attempt to escape from England, we were betrayed by the ship's captain, arrested, imprisoned, and all our goods confiscated. But once released, we went back to work, saved our money, and attempted it again. This time, we were successful.

NARRATOR TWO: The shores of Holland with their majestic windmills turning in the breeze must have been quite a sight to the persecuted Pilgrims! Here at last they could be free!

NARRATOR ONE: Life in Holland was hard for the Pilgrims. To earn enough money to live, every member of the Pilgrims' group—men, women, and children—had to labor from dawn until dusk.

BRADFORD: Holland was not the new home we were hoping for. Holland *was* tolerant, but it was not a holy land. We were shocked by the vulgar customs of the people and the coarse language we heard. Tolerance had brought religious freedom, but also religious looseness. We longed for a new society—one based on Biblical principles.

NARRATOR ONE: They knew they had to keep searching for an ideal home. But where else could they go? It was about that time that their thoughts turned to the New World.

BRADFORD: The New World! A savage wilderness! An unknown continent filled with wild men! It seemed like madness to some. But where else could we start a new society? Where else could we be a city on a hill—an example to all around us?

NARRATOR TWO: The countries of Europe were founding new colonies in the vast wilderness of America. The Old World held no hope for the Pilgrims. Therefore, they turned to the New World.

NARRATOR ONE: After spending twelve years in Holland, the Pilgrims finally saved enough money to charter a ship to the New World. They hoped to found their own colony near the Jamestown settlement. Maybe there they could find the religious freedom they desired.

BRADFORD: We could not afford the voyage on our own, so we joined together with a group of English travelers, seeking the New World for their own reasons. We called ourselves "saints" and them "strangers." Unfortunately, they were not happy to be spending months at sea with a group of religious zealots.

NARRATOR TWO: After a false start where a faulty ship called the *Speedwell* caused them to abort their voyage, 102 passengers embarked from England on a ship called the *Mayflower* headed for the Jamestown settlement in the New World.

NARRATOR ONE: Yet, even at the outset, the voyage was unfavorable. They were embarking with their food supply depleted. They were starting late in the season—August. 3,000 miles of Atlantic Ocean lay between them and their destination.

BRADFORD: You cannot imagine what it was like on that ship. The hold, where we spent our days, was only seventy-five feet long and not quite five feet high. We were all crammed in there—men, women, and children. And we were all sick. We were not used to the rough waves of the sea. The waves rolled over the sides of the ship, and the salt water sprayed down through the deck-boards upon us.

(sounds of crashing waves, creaking timbers, and wailing children)

BRADFORD: What made things worse was that the sailors onboard the *Mayflower* mocked our sickness. They considered us to be a bunch of crazed religious fanatics—and worse, landlubbers.

SAILOR: Can't stand a little rocking, huh? What a bunch of holy fools! Are you offended by the waves? Why don't you pray to God to calm them for you? *(laugh)* Ha!

BRADFORD: One of the sailors was the worst of the lot, and he cursed us with profane language. When we gently rebuked him, he only cursed us more.

SAILOR: Half of you will be dead soon from sickness. And then I'll laugh when I throw your dead bodies over into the sea. You'll make nice food for the crabs! And then I'll get to claim your possessions as my own! *(laugh)*

BRADFORD: But as the days passed, my people grew used to the lurching of the ship, and it was that young man—not us—who grew ill. At last he grew so ill that he died, and it was his body that was cast overboard first.

(splashing sound)

NARRATOR TWO: The rest of the sailors took this as a sign of God's punishment on the young man and no longer harassed the Pilgrims.

BRADFORD: As we passed across the sea, violent sea-storms assailed the ship. We were thrown turbulently around.

(sounds of a violent storm)

CAPTAIN: There's nothing else I can do! I must lower the sails, or we will lose them!

BRADFORD: We watched the captain lower the sails.

CAPTAIN: Now we are completely at the mercy of the storm.

BRADFORD: But that is where he was wrong. We were completely in God's hands then. For days the sails were not raised, and the winds blew us where they willed.

(whooshing sounds of wind)

BRADFORD: The sailors cursed, the strangers fretted, but we Pilgrims—we prayed and trusted that God would lead us.

NARRATOR ONE: One young Pilgrim, John Howland, who was on deck during one of the many storms, was lost overboard when the ship lurched to the side.

HOWLAND: *(screaming)* Ah! Brothers! Help me!

BRADFORD: God was watching over John Howland though. As he flew into the sea, John grasped at one of the loose sail ropes. The raging sea dragged John down ten feet beneath the water, but all the time he hung onto the rope. Gradually, we men hauled in the rope, bit by bit. Then at last John emerged from the waves—gasping for breath—but alive. God had preserved him.

HOWLAND: *(gasping for breath)* Thank you!

BRADFORD: Through this constant tossing back and forth of the sea-storms, one of the main beams of the ship's hold snapped like a chicken bone. *(cracking sound)* The captain feared that we would have to sail back to England for repairs.

CAPTAIN: The main beam is cracked. She won't hold for the rest of the voyage.

BRADFORD: But God had made provision for us. One of my people had brought a large screw-jack for constructing houses, and we were able to use this to prop up the beam—securing it, saving the ship, and preserving the voyage. It was God's will that we continue.

NARRATOR ONE: The unfavorable conditions slowed the Pilgrims' progress, and as the *Mayflower*'s journey dragged on, conditions aboard went from bad to worse. Food supplies ran low. The firewood was gone—and with it all warmth. The passengers had drunk their water barrels to the dregs. Soon there would be no fresh water. Those aboard began to show signs of malnutrition and scurvy—rancid breath, bleeding gums, and loosening teeth. The ship's medical officer was in constant demand. *(wailing of children)*

NARRATOR TWO: Then the first one of the Pilgrims died—a young boy who grew ill and never recovered. They all knew that they needed to reach the New World soon.

BRADFORD: Three women had been pregnant when we began the voyage. One gave birth in the midst of the sea, and she named her new son, Oceanus, after the rocking waves that accompanied his birth. A blessing of new life had brought a ray of light in our dark voyage.

NARRATOR ONE: Finally, after sixty-six grueling days at sea, over two months of sickness, the Pilgrims caught their first sight of land. It was America!

NARRATOR TWO: America! It would be called sweet land of liberty for years to come. For those weary Pilgrims, it must have been a beautiful sight! But even more amazing was what it symbolized—freedom to worship God as they wished.

BRADFORD: We could smell the land before we saw it. Land has a scent, you know. The water was pale green, and sea gulls filled the sky. We saw those giant, sandy cliffs and behind them nothing but virgin forest. No sight ever looked so good! We saw freedom there!

NARRATOR ONE: The Pilgrims had made it to the New World. But it was November 11, 1620, and winter was almost upon them. Also, they had sailed too far north—missing Jamestown by hundreds of miles. They were nearly out of food, and the forest that loomed ahead might be filled with bloodthirsty natives.

BRADFORD: We had heard many stories of the wild men of the New World—many brutal murders at the hands of these savages.

NARRATOR TWO: In preparation for any encounters with the natives, the passengers on the *Mayflower* had hired a military officer named Miles Standish to accompany them.

STANDISH: I will lead a party of men to scout out a safe spot for us to go ashore. If I encounter any of the savages, I will give them a taste of my musket!

NARRATOR ONE: Before the scouting party went ashore, some of the passengers insisted that there be a written contract among them—some compact that bound them all together.

BRADFORD: We are not in Jamestown, so we will have to form our own settlement. We will need rules to govern us.

NARRATOR ONE: So the *Mayflower* passengers drafted the Mayflower Compact, a document that outlined their duties and obligations. It gave them the power to decide their own laws and elect their leaders.

BRADFORD: *(reading)* In the presence of God and one another, we covenant and combine ourselves together into a civil body politic.

NARRATOR TWO: Over a hundred years later the founding fathers of America would look back to that document as the first declaration of democracy among the people of America.

NARRATOR ONE: Having drafted and agreed upon the Mayflower Compact, a party of the ship's leaders went ashore. Bradford was among those who went to scout out a safe landing spot, but when he returned to the ship, he was greeted by heartbreaking news.

BRADFORD: My fellow travelers informed me that my wife, Dorothy, had slipped and fallen from the moored ship—and drowned in the harbor.

NARRATOR TWO: Some of the other Pilgrims whispered that Dorothy had jumped intentionally. Her dreams of an earthly paradise and the grim reality of the sandy hills of Cape Cod had caused her to despair. After surviving the perils of the sea, Bradford had lost the one closest to him. In spite of his loss, he penned these words in his journal…

BRADFORD: Faint not, poor soul. In God still trust.

NARRATOR ONE: At last the ship harbored, and the Pilgrims went ashore—at a place now called Plymouth Rock. There they fell upon their knees and blessed the God of Heaven, who had brought them over the vast and furious ocean. He had set their feet back on solid ground—their proper element. They were thankful to be alive, but it was only then that a new truth sank in. They were in a new world—left to cope by themselves.

BRADFORD: There were no inns to welcome us. No friends to greet us. Before us lay a savage wilderness, filled with wild men and beasts. Behind us lay the width of the ocean. There was nothing—nothing—to sustain us—but the Spirit of God.

NARRATOR TWO: The next three months spelled the darkest time of the Pilgrim's journey. Harsh wintery conditions came on quickly. The *Mayflower*, still harbored in the bay, offered the only shelter for the women and children, while the men struggled to build homes upon the shore from timber and mud. *(sounds of construction)*

NARRATOR ONE: Journeying back and forth though the frigid water spelled the doom of many of the men. Pneumonia beset the Pilgrims—along with malnutrition and the diseases they still suffered from the sea.

NARRATOR TWO: At last all work ceased, and they huddled in the ship—Pilgrims and strangers alike—fighting sickness and the cold conditions. Death began to take its toll.

BRADFORD: We were forced to lay many of our own—men, women, and children—in cold graves. Some days two or three died at a time.

NARRATOR ONE: Their numbers began to dwindle. It looked like their journey would end in defeat. So many of the passengers became ill that there were only six left among them healthy enough to care for the others.

BRADFORD: It was God who held these men up from sickness. These six bravely risked their own health to care for the others—wading ashore for firewood, changing the loathsome clothes of the sick, and tending to the needs of all the passengers, not just their fellow Pilgrims. Some of the strangers were driven to tears by the kind acts of these pilgrims.

STRANGER: If our roles were reversed, we would have let you die like dogs, but I see that you are true Christians. You care for each other. You care for us. I am not worthy of it! Thank you!

BRADFORD: One hundred of us had landed in the New World, but by the end of that winter, only fifty survived. But our struggles bonded us together. We were no longer two groups—saints and strangers. By the end of that winter, we were all Pilgrims.

NARRATOR TWO: The winter took a staggering toll. 102 had crossed the ocean. Three months later only fifty-two survived.

NARRATOR ONE: When the winter seemed the darkest, it finally broke. As spring came on, the Pilgrims were free to observe the beauty of the New World they had journeyed so far to see. The templed hills of America came to life with springtime, and all nature sang around them.

NARRATOR TWO: After practically starving through the winter months, the Pilgrims were determined not to face another winter unprepared. But they knew nothing about farming in the New World. The crops of the old world failed here. It looked like starvation would claim them once the cold seasons came again.

NARRATOR ONE: Throughout the winter, the Pilgrims frequently caught glimpses of the Native Americans—away in the trees, watching them curiously, like phantoms of the forest. Miles Standish kept a wary eye upon the natives.

STANDISH: Bury your dead in unmarked graves. We cannot have the savages see how few our numbers are.

BRADFORD: As the winter began to slacken, we moved into the few houses we had been able to build before the sickness overtook us and our families. Captain Standish aimed his cannons toward the forest—anticipating an Indian attack.

STANDISH: Mark my words! Those savages will come when we are at our weakest point!

NARRATOR TWO: Captain Standish was right. The Indians did come when the Pilgrims were at their weakest point. But not as expected.

NARRATOR ONE: One day, a lone Indian warrior walked boldly into the middle of the Pilgrim settlement. The nervous Pilgrims gathered around him—wondering what his intentions were.

BRADFORD: I had never seen a man so tall and straight. His hair was long in back, cut short in the front, and black as midnight. He began walking directly toward us. The guards sounded the alarm, and all the men ran outdoors, but the Indian kept walking. He walked directly into our village. We thought he might walk directly into one of our homes—he was so bold!

NARRATOR TWO: At last the Indian stopped, saluted those there, and greeted them in their own language:

SAMOSET: Welcome, Englishmen!

BRADFORD: Can you imagine our shock to hear our own language spoken by this wild man? He told us much. His name was Samoset, and the chief who ruled this region was called Massasoit.

NARRATOR ONE: As Samoset continued to converse with the Pilgrims into the evening, it became clear that he wished to stay with them for the night. The Indian was allowed to bunk in with the Hopkins family.

BRADFORD: It was an odd beginning to this New World that we never expected! A nearly naked savage bunking in one of our own houses!

NARRATOR TWO: Samoset promised to return in a few days with the sachem or chief, Massasoit. He also promised to bring along an Indian who spoke even better English than he did—one named Squanto.

BRADFORD: There was the usual distrust. How could we be sure that this had not been a trap? What if the Indians did not return in peace? A few days later when Chief Massasoit did arrive with sixty warriors, I'm sure many of us did fear for our lives.

NARRATOR ONE: The Indians arrived with their faces painted—some red, some yellow, some black, some white. Massasoit's face was painted red—a necklace of sea-shells hanging around his neck and a knife dangling from his belt. *(murmuring of the Pilgrims)*

NARRATOR TWO: The Indian leader and his warriors appeared every bit the savages that the stories had cast them. But they came in peace. The Pilgrim governor greeted them as dignitaries—inviting them into their village, kissing the chief's hand, offering them food and drink.

BRADFORD: It was then that I met the man who has become my dearest friend—Squanto. Because of his gift of translation, we were able to communicate with the chief. We developed a treaty of peace.

NARRATOR TWO: The terms of the treaty were simple. None of the Indians would do any harm to the Pilgrims. If any Indian did hurt a white man, the offender would be turned over to the Pilgrims for punishment. If anything were stolen from the Pilgrims, the Indians would restore it to them. If any enemy made war against Massasoit's tribe, the Pilgrims would aid him. It was a treaty that was honored by both sides over the many years of Massasoit's reign.

BRADFORD: We came to the New World expecting savages. Instead, we found a people who were trustworthy, witty, and just.

NARRATOR ONE: Finally, in April of that year, the *Mayflower* and its crew sailed back to England. It is a testament to the people's solidarity that not one of the passengers left with it. They had resolved to stay in the New World—no matter what. The Pilgrims elected William Bradford as their governor because he was a person of piety, wisdom, and courage.

BRADFORD: That summer, my friend Squanto came to live with us. He was the instrument of God. He told me the fascinating story of how he had come to know so many of the white man's ways.

SQUANTO: I was abducted from my home and taken to the land of the white man, England—as a slave. That is how I learned your language. But I escaped from slavery and returned home. Then I was captured again and sold as a slave in Spain. But again I escaped and returned to my homeland. Yet when I arrived, I learned that my tribe had vanished. They once lived here where you now live. This was once my home. Now it is again. I live with you.

NARRATOR TWO: Squanto showed the Pilgrims the best places to fish and demonstrated the technique of catching eels.

BRADFORD: Squanto arrived with a load of eels so large that he could barely support it!

NARRATOR ONE: Most importantly, Squanto showed them the use of Indian corn.

SQUANTO: For my people, planting is the women's work, but I know enough of it to show you. Catching the fish is much needed for your crops to thrive. You must bury the fish with your corn seeds—to fertilize the soil in your mound.

NARRATOR TWO: During this time, William Bradford and Squanto formed a friendship that would last a lifetime. Because of Squanto's help, the crops of the Pilgrims thrived, and they stored up supplies so that they would be ready for the next winter.

NARRATOR ONE: When autumn arrived, the trees changed color with a vibrancy the Pilgrims had never witnessed in England. It was the perfect end to an arduous year. God had given them a gift—and it was a gift to be shared.

BRADFORD: After the harvest that year, we summoned Massasoit and some of his warriors for a celebratory feast. We wished to rejoice together after a more special manner. We wished them to share in the fruit of our labor. We ate harvested corn, squash, beans, barley, and peas. We served duck, geese, and wild turkey. The Indians brought freshly killed deer. Massasoit brought one hundred warriors with him, and our feasting made quite a scene. We sat upon rocks, stumps, or the ground and ate our bounty. But we were peaceful and joyful and thankful.

NARRATOR TWO: No one recorded the exact date of this first Thanksgiving, but it was probably in late September or early October of 1621. No one knew it was a scene that would be re-enacted throughout the years.

NARRATOR ONE: Squanto never left the Pilgrims—even until the day he died. As he died, he called for his friend, William Bradford.

SQUANTO: Pray for me—that I may go to the Englishmen's God—in Heaven. I leave to you my possessions as a remembrance of me.

BRADFORD: My friend, Squanto had taken sick with a fever. His death was a great loss.

NARRATOR TWO: In the New World, among a race they had once distrusted, the Pilgrims had discovered a faithful friend.

BRADFORD: When I look back on our voyage to the New World, I see the hand of God at work—in every instance. Because of the help of the Indians, our Plymouth settlement survived. It went on to be a city on a hill for all others to emulate.

NARRATOR ONE: Four hundred years later, we still celebrate these devout forefathers—as we dwell in a country founded upon the principle of religious freedom. The Pilgrims and their amazing journey serve as a reminder that…

BRADFORD: All great and honorable actions are accompanied with great difficulties, and both must be enterprised and overcome with answerable courage.

DISCUSSION QUESTIONS

1. You have probably heard this story before. Listening to the story this time, did you learn something new? Explain.
2. What is amazing about the Pilgrims' journey? Explain.
3. What part did the Pilgrims' faith play in their journey?
4. Why is the Mayflower Compact an important document in American history?

5. How important was the friendship between the Pilgrims and the Native Americans?
6. Judging by the peace treaty between the Pilgrims and the Indians, what did both sides have to gain?
7. What is amazing about Squanto's life story?
8. Fifty years after the Pilgrims landed, New England would be torn apart by war between the Indians and European settlers. How does this contrast with the way the Pilgrims and Indians first interacted?
9. Religious freedom has always been one of America's highest ideals. The founding fathers looked back to the Pilgrims as the basis for their legislation protecting freedom of religion. How important are the Pilgrims in our history? Explain.

THE COURTSHIP OF MILES STANDISH
TEACHER GUIDE

BACKGROUND

Life in the New World for the Puritan Pilgrims revolved around family and faith. Adhering to their Puritan beliefs, they sought to live a good and holy life that would be pleasing to God. Although the stereotype of the Puritans is that they were cold and unfeeling (not romantic types at all), they were actually proponents of "true love." Arranged marriages were still common in England, but Puritans instead stressed a deep, personal love in marriage. In fact, the modern idea of *true love* is one that Puritans would agree with.

That being said, the Puritans still had strict rules for courting. Young Puritans were never to be left alone with the opposite sex unsupervised nor in close physical proximity. They were expected to "date" in a crowded room of other family members. One tool that allowed these young Puritans to have a private conversation was something called a "courting stick," a long, hollow stick that the young people could use to whisper messages to one another from several feet away.

Henry Wadsworth Longfellow's famous poem *The Courtship of Miles Standish* portrays a Puritan love triangle, one he claimed was based on actual history. All members of the love triangle (John Alden, Priscilla Mullens, and Miles Standish) are true historical figures. In fact, Longfellow was a descendant of John Alden and Priscilla Mullens. He claimed that this story was a family legend passed down through the generations. This script-story is based on Longfellow's famous narrative poem.

SUMMARY

John Alden is one of the Pilgrims, who have just arrived in America, and he has fallen secretly in love with a Pilgrim woman named Priscilla Mullens. Being incredibly shy, John cannot voice his love, although he pays frequent visits to Priscilla's house. John's best friend and father-figure is Miles Standish, the military officer of the Pilgrims. One day Standish asks John to do a great favor for him—ask Priscilla Mullens to be his wife. John is immediately conflicted since he loves Priscilla himself but decides to put the interest of his friend before his.

John goes to Priscilla's home and tells Priscilla he has come to propose to her for Standish. Priscilla is surprised by this, so John begins to tell her all about the great qualities of Standish. Finally, Priscilla stops and commands John to tell her why *he* should be her husband instead. John realizes the truth—Priscilla loves *him*—and leaves hurriedly.

John breaks the bad news to Standish, who explodes in anger and accuses John of betraying him. Heartbroken by this, John considers returning to England with the *Mayflower*, yet he decides to stay near Priscilla. Since John knows that his friend loves Priscilla, he will not pursue a relationship with her.

Soon after this, Standish goes to fight in an Indian war, and a report comes back that he was killed by an Indian warrior. John, instead of being heartbroken by this news, is overjoyed since it means he can marry Priscilla. The happy couple plans their wedding, but on their wedding day Standish returns. Reports of his death were greatly exaggerated. John expects Standish to be angry at the wedded couple, but Standish instead gives them his blessing.

ESSENTIAL QUESTIONS

- What should be the basis for love?
- Why is it important to have effective communication?

CONNECT

***The Courtship of Miles Standish* by Henry Wadsworth Longfellow** Written in 1858, this narrative poem fondly remembers the early American Puritan time period. Its sentimental style is common among Romantic poets of the day, of whom Longfellow was the foremost. Read the poem and compare it to this script-story adaptation.

ANTICIPATORY QUESTIONS

- Who were the Pilgrims?
- Have you ever been afraid to tell someone how you really feel about him or her?
- Have you ever made a sacrifice for a friend?

TEACHABLE TERMS

- **Narrative Poem** *The Courtship of Miles Standish*, the poem upon which this script-story is based, is an example of a narrative poem or a poem that tells a story. Read the original poem and compare it to this adaptation.
- **Simile/Metaphor** On pg. 64 the text says that John's heart "leapt like a deer," which is an example of a simile. On pg. 70 Priscilla calls Miles Standish a "little chimney," an example of a metaphor.
- **Idiom** On pg. 65 Priscilla says before John gets around to proposing, she will be an old "thornback," an idiom meaning an older, unmarried woman.

- **Inner Conflict** John Alden is torn between two affections: his friendship with Miles Standish and his love for Priscilla Mullens. This leads to an inner conflict, which is mentioned on pgs. 66-67.
- **Dramatic Irony** Throughout the poem, we know of John's love for Priscilla; however, we are unsure if she knows of this love or not. This dramatic tension leads to a payoff when Priscilla tells John that he should speak for himself on pg. 68, indicating that she knows his true feelings for her.
- **Situational Irony** On pgs. 71-72 when Miles Standish returns after being presumed dead, the reader expects him to be angry when he shows up at the wedding of John and Priscilla. His reaction, however, is the opposite of what the reader expects.

RECALL QUESTIONS

1. What can John Alden not tell Priscilla Mullens?
2. What secret does Miles Standish tell John Alden?
3. According to a false report, how does Miles Standish die?
4. What is John Alden's reaction to the news of Miles Standish's death?
5. Who is a surprise guest at John and Priscilla's wedding?

THE COURTSHIP OF MILES STANDISH

ADAPTED FROM THE POEM BY HENRY WADSWORTH LONGFELLOW

CAST

STANDISH	*Plymouth's Military Officer*
JOHN	*Young Plymouth Man*
PRISCILLA	*Young Plymouth Woman*
BRADFORD	*Governor of Plymouth*
WOMAN	*Woman of Plymouth*
BOY	*Young Man of Plymouth*

NARRATOR: In Plymouth, the land of the Pilgrims, the *Mayflower* rocked majestically in the bay. The ship's sails, which had hung in tatters all winter, were now mended and unfurled—catching the beckoning breeze. All was prepared for the great vessel to make its return voyage to its homeland, England.

Watching the ship from a high hill was a young Pilgrim man named John Alden. As he gazed out over the bay, his azure eyes were full of the dew of youth.

JOHN: Farewell, blessed ship. I will forever be in your debt.

NARRATOR: Although part of the Pilgrims now, John Alden had not come to the New World for the same reasons as the Pilgrims. He had been hired as one of the ship's crewmen to make repairs to the *Mayflower* upon its voyage.

JOHN: Who knew that you, noble craft, would show me the love of my life?

NARRATOR: Upon the voyage to the New World, John Alden had seen the fearless faith of the Pilgrims and had become one of their number. Yet it was one Pilgrim, above all the others, who had prompted this change of heart and his desire to remain in the New World.

JOHN: Without you I would have never met Priscilla. *(sigh)* Well, enough daydreaming.

NARRATOR: Also among the Pilgrim settlers was a young woman named Priscilla Mullens, who had voyaged upon the *Mayflower* with her mother, father, and siblings. During the previous harsh winter, sickness had claimed the rest of her family, and now she lived in their house alone except for a nearly-deaf, old widow, who was her only companion.

JOHN: Perhaps I will look in upon Priscilla— just to make sure she does not need some kind of assistance.

NARRATOR: John Alden rose and made his way toward the cottage of Priscilla Mullens. Although he dared not admit it to anyone but himself, he was desperately in love with her.

Being an incredibly shy man, who did not speak much unless in the presence of his closest companions, John was well-skilled in words, and this talent had landed him the occupation of assistant to William Bradford, the governor of Plymouth Colony. He earned enough of a living to support a wife, yet he could never find the words that needed to be spoken to his one, true love.

JOHN: Perhaps today will be the day!

NARRATOR: John arrived at Priscilla's cottage and nervously knocked upon the door. When the young woman answered the door, John fumbled with his hat in his hands.

PRISCILLA: John Alden!

JOHN: *(nervously)* W-w-would you mind if I came in to sit for a bit, Miss Mullens?

NARRATOR: The young woman showed him inside. Her elderly roommate snored open-mouthed beside the fire. *(snoring of an old woman)* They seated themselves, and Priscilla picked up her sewing.

PRISCILLA: I will not dare to say that I am surprised by your visit.

JOHN: You won't?

PRISCILLA: I knew it was you from the moment I heard your step coming up the path. You have a very distinct step, you know. But even before that I was thinking of you as I sat here singing and sewing.

JOHN: Y-y-you were thinking of me?

NARRATOR: John's heart leapt like a deer. Perhaps she held feelings for him as well.

PRISCILLA: I was remembering that day last winter when the snows came so heavily. You cleared a path from the edge of the village to my cottage. You sure had snowy locks when you finally came inside! *(laugh)* You looked quite like an old man. My roommate might have made eyes with you—if she had been conscious.

NARRATOR: John smiled bashfully.

PRISCILLA: But what business brings you here today?

JOHN: *(nervously)* Did you know, Miss Mullens, I was not one of the Pilgrims when I came aboard the *Mayflower*? I was hired as a carpenter.

PRISCILLA: I know, John. I thought you were quite a heathen.

JOHN: Well, maybe…a bit. *(nervous laugh)* But upon the voyage something changed. There was something so amazing about you—I mean, your people!

PRISCILLA: Something amazing? About me—or my people?

JOHN: Both! I mean…*(cough)*

NARRATOR: John was fidgeting so roughly with his hat that Priscilla feared he would tear it in half.

JOHN: I said all of that to say—it seems prudent that you—and me—I mean, we—should…*(cough)*

NARRATOR: Priscilla stopped her sewing and looked up at John hopefully.

PRISCILLA: If you have something to say, by all means, say it!

JOHN: Well, I...*(cough)* I had better be going.

NARRATOR: John crammed his hat back onto his head and disappeared out the door as quickly as he had come. Priscilla shrugged and returned to her sewing.

PRISCILLA: *(sigh)* I will be an old thornback before that man finally asks me to marry him.

NARRATOR: Returning along the forest path, John Alden crossly confronted himself.

JOHN: You coward! You boob! Why can you not speak the words? You obviously adore the woman! Tell her! *(pause)* Tomorrow! I will do it tomorrow for sure!

NARRATOR: John's steps turned toward his own home. Ever since arriving in the New World, John had been the roommate of Miles Standish, the Pilgrims' military officer. John had no family, and Captain Standish's wife had died during the long winter. Sharing a home had made them fast friends.

With his mind still reeling with torturous thoughts, John entered the crudely-built cabin he and Standish shared only to find his roommate in a state of agitation as well. The captain was stalking back and forth, buried in thought with his hands clasped behind his back. He let out hearty sighs like a teapot puffing out steam.

STANDISH: *(huffing and puffing)* Hmph! Hmph! Hmph!

NARRATOR: Standish was short of stature but strongly built and athletic—broad in the shoulders, deep-chested, with muscles and sinews of iron. He had some age as well. His russet beard was already flaked with patches of snow—as hedges will be sometimes in November.

JOHN: Good evening, Captain.

STANDISH: Hmmmm.

NARRATOR: John Alden seated himself at the table by the window to collect his thoughts. He pulled out his pen and began to write. As always, no matter what subject upon which he intended to write, there was only one subject that came forth—Priscilla.

STANDISH: *(extremely long sigh)*

NARRATOR: With a final hiss of steam, Captain Standish came to a stop by the window that looked out over the Pilgrim encampment.

STANDISH: My friend, John. Look yonder there! On the hill by the sea lies Rose Standish—my rose. She was one of the first to die in this long, frightful winter.

JOHN: I know, my friend.

STANDISH: Her grave is not marked. That was my choice, you know. We dared not mark the graves, or the red men in the forest would have seen how many of us perished during this winter. But one day I will make her a fine marker. I still remember the spot. How could I forget?

JOHN: We shall make it together, my friend. It is worthy that such a wonderful wife be remembered.

STANDISH: The Bible says that it is not good that man be alone.

NARRATOR: These words only made the pang in John's heart hurt deeper.

JOHN: I agree, my friend.

NARRATOR: Captain Standish turned to an old, burnished breastplate that hung upon the wall and pointed to a dent upon it.

STANDISH: See there! That was caused by a bullet aimed at my heart by a Spanish mercenary. Ha! In that battle I charged at the head of my men. It has always been my motto to do things myself and not leave it to others.

JOHN: Praise God that He sent His breath to slow that bullet, or I would have lost my greatest friend!

STANDISH: Hmmm. Of late, I have been reading of Julius Caesar and his mighty campaigns. A wonderful man was he. You, John Alden, are a writer. I am a fighter. But Caesar, he was a writer *and* a fighter. He conquered his enemies and then wrote about his victories in lofty prose.

JOHN: What is the point in all of this? Is there something on your mind, my friend?

STANDISH: I cannot interrupt your work.

JOHN: This is not work. I am merely writing epistles to send back to England with the *Mayflower* when it embarks. There is nothing more important than what you have to say.

NARRATOR: As the young man put down his writing, the aging war-leader turned and looked into his eyes.

STANDISH: Although I have said that it is always best to do things yourself, I am afraid I must ask you a favor.

JOHN: (*happily*) Anything! You have been like a father to me! I do not know what would have happened if you had not taken me under your wing. You gave me this home and your friendship! Just ask the request, and I will do it.

STANDISH: Since my Rose died, my life has been weary and dreary. Sick at heart I have been, but of late I have felt my spirit stirred again by—I feel so foolish to say it—a maiden of our colony.

JOHN: There is nothing foolish about that. It is the purpose of every heart to love. Who is the woman in question?

STANDISH: The young Priscilla Mullens.

NARRATOR: John Alden felt his heart grow cold.

STANDISH: As your friend, I ask you—go to Priscilla, the loveliest maiden in Plymouth, and say that old Captain Standish offers his hand and heart to her—the hand and heart of a soldier.

NARRATOR: John could not even stammer out a response.

STANDISH: Surely you won't refuse me! While I am valiant in most matters, I am a coward when it comes to things like this! I am a maker of war—not phrases. Go and woo her with words that you think are best adapted to win her heart. I'm not afraid of a blast from the mouth of a cannon! But I am terrified of a thundering "No!" fired point-blank from the mouth of a woman.

NARRATOR: He took the hand of his young friend.

STANDISH: Surely you cannot refuse what I ask in the name of our friendship.

The Courtship of Miles Standish

NARRATOR: So the strong will prevailed, and John Alden went on his grim errand. It was as if he were joining in the funeral march of all his dreams. He inched down the muddy road through the dwellings of Plymouth and into the paths of the forest—his love contending with friendship in his heart. He cursed his timidity—his inability to speak to one who was now spoken for.

As he passed through the woods, the May flowers were blooming. He stooped low to the ground, picked a blossom, and examined it pensively.

JOHN: This flower reminds me of her—modest, simple, and sweet. I will take it to her as a parting gift. Then it will be thrown away—just like the heart of the giver.

NARRATOR: At long last John reached Priscilla's cottage. He knocked, and as her friendly voice beckoned him within, he beheld her seated at her spinning wheel. *(whirring of a spinning wheel)* The carded wool was like a snow drift piled at her knee, her beautiful hands were feeding the wool into the ravenous spindle, and her foot on the treadle guided the wheel in its motion. It nearly broke his heart to behold her.

PRISCILLA: Mr. Alden? Back so soon?

JOHN: I—I—brought you these.

NARRATOR: He held out the May flowers.

PRISCILLA: Beautiful! So simple and sweet. So what brings you back here? Apart from flower-picking, that is.

NARRATOR: As he opened his mouth to speak, John did not know which would come out—a profession of his own love or that of Captain Standish.

JOHN: I—er...*(cough)*

PRISCILLA: Perhaps I can speak first. I have been thinking. The *Mayflower* is set to sail back to England. I thought that perhaps I should be upon it.

NARRATOR: She slyly looked up to see the young man's reaction. His face had gone as white as her wool.

JOHN: *(shocked)* Whatever for?

PRISCILLA: Oh, I was remembering the hedgerows of England. I do miss them, you know. Plus, it is so lonely and wretched here. *(pause)* You know, with me living all alone...by myself...except for my aged companion, of course.

JOHN: You are right. You have such a tender and trusting heart. You need a stronger one to lean on from time to time. That is why I have come.

PRISCILLA: *(excitedly)* Yes, John?

JOHN: I have come with an offer of marriage made by a man good and true.

NARRATOR: A look of delight washed over Priscilla's face.

PRISCILLA: And what might the name of this good man be?

JOHN: Miles Standish, the Captain of Plymouth.

NARRATOR: Priscilla recoiled in confusion as if John's words were a blow that had struck her. Then she simply turned back to her spinning. *(whirring of a spinning wheel)*

JOHN: Miss Mullens? What is your answer?

PRISCILLA: *(angrily)* If the great Captain of Plymouth is so very eager to wed me, why does he not come himself and woo me? If I am not worth the wooing, I am surely not worth the winning!

NARRATOR: John Alden began to stammer and stumble over himself.

JOHN: Oh, the captain is so busy. He has no time for such things.

PRISCILLA: Oh really? If he has no time for "such things," as you call them, *before* marriage, I can imagine how little time he would have *after* our marriage. That is the way with men.

JOHN: My friend loves you with all his heart and must have an answer.

PRISCILLA: Well, you can speak more with actions than words. You should know that by now, John. Go back and tell your puppetmaster, this old and rough captain of yours, that if he had *showed* that he loved me, he might have won me.

NARRATOR: Feeling his duty to his friend welling up within him, overpowering his own desires, John Alden began to tell Priscilla all the merits of Miles Standish—his courage and skills, the many battles he had won.

PRISCILLA: Why is war supposed to inspire my love?

JOHN: But with a gentle hand he attended the sick during this long winter!

PRISCILLA: He attended a bedside? I'm surprised he could reach it as short as he is!

JOHN: You wrong him! Do not laugh and scorn him because of his little stature. Any woman in Plymouth—no, all of England—would be proud to be the wife of Miles Standish.

NARRATOR: John had warmed and glowed as he spoke his friend's suit to Priscilla in his simple and elegant language. Now Priscilla began to smirk—laughter dancing in her eyes. She stopped her spinning and stared John straight in the face.

PRISCILLA: Now that you have spoken for him, why don't you speak for yourself, John? Tell me why I should be happy to be *your* wife instead. That is the suit I want to hear.

JOHN: W-w-what? How can you speak out so plainly?

PRISCILLA: I am only saying the words that you cannot! Is it the fate of a woman to wait like a speechless ghost until asked a question? If I waited for you to ask me on your own, I would be waiting forever. It is no secret—I would love to be with you, to see you, to speak with you always. John, you're the one I want!

JOHN: I must go—at once!

NARRATOR: Perplexed and bewildered, John Alden jumped up and rushed out of the cottage.

JOHN: *(in despair)* I did my duty! But in spite of all that, she chose me! Is that my fault?

NARRATOR: As John Alden walked by the bay, he uplifted his head and saw the shadow of the *Mayflower* anchored there. He heard the voice of the men through the mist preparing the vessel to sail.

JOHN: Once I tell Captain Standish this news, he will no longer be my friend. And I would never betray him by taking Priscilla against his wishes. Yes, it is plain to me. There is only one course of action. I must return back to England. I will go back over the ocean and abandon this dreary land.

NARRATOR: Finally, John made it back to his home, which he reluctantly entered. Miles Standish jumped up when John appeared.

STANDISH: *(laughing)* Ha! It took you long enough on this errand! I could have fought ten battles and sacked a city in the same amount of time! Tell me all that happened.

NARRATOR: John sat his friend down and told him all that transpired. He tried to smooth over the startling news—that Priscilla Mullens preferred humble John Alden to mighty Miles Standish. But there is no smoothing some news. When the aging captain heard this, he leapt up and stamped down his mighty foot.

STANDISH: *(roaring)* What? John Alden, how could you? You have supplanted, defrauded, and betrayed me!

JOHN: That is not so!

STANDISH: *(bellowing)* Silence!

NARRATOR: Miles Standish bellowed so loudly that it rattled the armor hanging on the walls. *(rattling of armor)* The veins in his temples bulged out like tightly-pulled cords.

STANDISH: *(yelling)* What shall prevent me from running my sword through the heart of a traitor? I cherished and loved you as a brother—a son! Just like Brutus betrayed Caesar, you have betrayed me! Let there be nothing between us save war and implacable hatred!

NARRATOR: There is no telling what might have occurred if there had not been a knocking at the door. *(door knock)* Captain Standish nearly ripped the door from the hinges, and the startled Pilgrim boy behind it shrunk back at the sight of the enraged war leader.

BOY: S-s-sir, it's the savages, sir. They have called on us to honor our treaty and fight alongside them against enemy tribes. The governor told me to come for you. Am I interrupting something?

NARRATOR: Standish turned to John Alden with a sneer.

STANDISH: No! There is nothing here that matters to me! Just a traitor!

NARRATOR: Standish grabbed his armor from the wall, furiously buckled it on, and disappeared from the cabin. *(door slamming)* John Alden hung his head in shame. Now he had lost everything—his friend and his love.

The day of the *Mayflower*'s departure arrived, and once again John Alden stood upon the hill overlooking the bay. In his hand he carried a sack, which contained his meager earthly belongings.

JOHN: Should I go? There is no way Priscilla will have me now. I have embarrassed and shamed her by fleeing from her presence.

NARRATOR: The sailors busied themselves in the rigging—preparing for the long journey. He remembered when he was just a crewman like them.

JOHN: But I know in my heart that there is no air so pure and so wholesome as the air she breathes—as the soil she walks. So here I will stay—just to watch over her. My foot was one of the first to step on this rock at the landing, and, God willing, it will be the last to leave.

NARRATOR: He stood there for hours, and finally he watched the ship hoist its sail and depart. It shimmered like the Spirit of God upon the waters. When he turned to return home, Priscilla was standing there.

PRISCILLA: I am glad you did not choose to go. You are not too offended to speak to me, are you?

JOHN: I do not know what to say.

PRISCILLA: Well, say something! Did you tell Captain Standish my message?

JOHN: I did, and he exploded with rage.

PRISCILLA: Let the little chimney puff all he wants. He won't have me. But I am still yours for the taking.

NARRATOR: John Alden sadly bowed his head.

JOHN: Yes, we will always be friends. But understand that we can never be more.

PRISCILLA: If all men had friends as loyal as you, the world would always be at peace. Very well, walk me back to my cottage.

NARRATOR: The days passed on. Little news reached the Plymouth settlement of Captain Standish's campaign in the Indian wars. Meanwhile, John Alden began to build his own habitation separate from Captain Standish. Ever of Priscilla he thought as he fashioned the walls and tilled the soil of the garden, and he mourned that she would never be the mistress of his home.

At the end of each day's labor, John went to the cottage of Priscilla, where she was frequently in the midst of her spinning. *(whirring of a spinning wheel)*

PRISCILLA: John! As you can see, I am being a model wife—spinning my wool. Perhaps you would like to be a model husband and hold the wool for me?

JOHN: Certainly. Certainly.

NARRATOR: He held out his hands, and she looped the ropes of wool around them.

PRISCILLA: How is your diminutive roommate?

JOHN: He has not returned. Recently word came that during peace talks with the enemy Indians, Captain Standish drove his knife into an Indian warrior's heart.

PRISCILLA: Oh my. I doubt that improved peace talks much. What caused such an outburst?

JOHN: The Indian mocked his height.

PRISCILLA: *(laughing)* Who wouldn't? The man is an elf. If he stabs everyone who would mock his height, we all would be in danger.

JOHN: Now the battle is on—thicker than ever. Who knows when he will return.

PRISCILLA: Hold your hands steady, John, or the thread will be tangled.

NARRATOR: As she expertly disentangled the thread from John's hands, she touched them lightly. Each time she did, it sent an electric thrill through every nerve in his body.

JOHN: Priscilla, I—

PRISCILLA: Yes?

NARRATOR: Just then there was a loud rapping at the door. *(door knocking sound)* Priscilla rose and answered it. The face of frightened boy stood behind it.

BOY: News from the Indian battle! Captain Standish has been killed!

PRISCILLA: What? How?

BOY: During battle, he was separated from his troops. An Indian scout brought word back that he was slain by a poisoned arrow.

NARRATOR: As the boy departed, Priscilla rushed to John's side to comfort him.

PRISCILLA: *(sadly)* Oh, John. I am so sorry! Your dear friend—dead!

NARRATOR: John stared blankly in stunned silence.

PRISCILLA: Say something, John! Your friend is slain!

NARRATOR: John's eyes suddenly cleared.

JOHN: *(happily)* Praise Heaven!

NARRATOR: He clasped Priscilla in his arms—pressing her close to his heart.

JOHN: Those God has united, let no man put asunder!

NARRATOR: As Plymouth mourned the passing of Captain Standish, the joyful announcement of a wedding was made. John Alden and Priscilla Mullens were to be joined in holy matrimony.

Soon the happy day arrived, and all the settlement gathered for the festive occasion. *(sounds of a happy gathering)* Governor William Bradford himself had agreed to perform the ceremony for the happy couple.

BRADFORD: By the power vested in me by the settlement of Plymouth and God Almighty, I pronounce you man and wife.

JOHN: Priscilla, you have made me the happiest man alive!

PRISCILLA: And you have made me the happiest woman!

NARRATOR: Just as the service ended and the wedded couple turned to exit the church, a dark form appeared in the doorway. All of the gathered guests turned and gasped. *(gasping of the crowd)* It was a grisly figure wearing bloodstained armor.

WOMAN: *(shrieking)* What is it? A ghost?

BRADFORD: *(breathlessly)* No! It is our Captain Standish—returned from the dead!

NARRATOR: It was true. Captain Standish was standing there—his body smeared with mud and filth.

JOHN: *(breathlessly)* Impossible!

NARRATOR: As the crowd stared in stunned silence, Standish stalked up the length of the church toward the wedded couple. John Alden did not shrink back but rose up even straighter than before. Coming to a stop before the newlyweds, Standish removed his helmet.

BRADFORD: Standish, they said you were dead.

STANDISH: They were wrong. When I heard of this wedding, I came here at once.

NARRATOR: He extended his hand toward John.

STANDISH: I wanted to be the first to congratulate you—my friend. I ask your forgiveness. It was small of me to ever doubt your loyalty.

JOHN: But—but—

STANDISH: Never so much as now is Miles Standish the friend of John Alden.

NARRATOR: John Alden threw his arms around the grizzled form of Standish.

STANDISH: Enough of that now. This is your wedding, my young friend. You must celebrate!

NARRATOR: Standish brushed John from him and turned to Priscilla—offering her a soldierly salute.

STANDISH: Now, I must depart. I would rather storm an Indian encampment than crash a wedding to which I was not invited.

JOHN: Nonsense! Stay, my friend! Celebrate with us!

PRISCILLA: Yes, captain. You would honor us with your presence.

STANDISH: Well, if you insist. I am a bit parched. *(shouting)* Let's feast!

NARRATOR: Great was the people's amazement to see their captain alive, but greater still was their rejoicing at the union of John Alden and Priscilla Mullens. It was an unexpected end to the courtship of Miles Standish.

DISCUSSION QUESTIONS

1. How is this story an example of a love triangle?
2. What is John Alden's inner conflict?
3. Would this have been a difficult choice for you to make? Explain.
4. How does Priscilla Mullens seem like a modern woman?
5. What parts of the story surprised you?

CAPTURED BY INDIANS
TEACHER GUIDE

BACKGROUND

Readers back in England were fascinated by the thought of the New World and the "savage" Indians who lived there, which explains why a Puritan woman's account of her capture by Indians became a runaway bestseller.

While relations between the New England Puritans and the local Indian tribes had begun peacefully, these relations soon broke down. Metacomet, nicknamed "King Philip" by the colonists, was the son of the Indian leader Massasoit, chief of the Wampanoag tribe who had made a treaty with the Pilgrims. In 1675 Metacomet led a group of Indian tribes in open war against the colonists. The Wampanoag tribe joined with the Nipmucks, Pocumtucks, and Narragansetts in a bloody uprising against the colonists. The reasons for this rebellion are debated, but the Indians had become increasingly dependent on English goods, food, and weapons. Tribal lands had been sold—forcing the Indians into smaller spaces, which restricted their ability to practice their traditional way of life. The war of King Philip was the Indian's last ditch effort to force European settlers out of America.

King Philip's War lasted fourteen months and destroyed twelve frontier towns. It is estimated that 1,000 colonists and 3,000 Indians died in the conflict. It was during this bloody conflict that Mary Rowlandson of Lancaster, Massachusetts was abducted and kept for ransom. The narrative she wrote about her captivity became a classic of American Literature. This script-story is an adaptation of her account.

SUMMARY

Mary Rowlandson and her family awake one night to find their town under attack by hostile Indians. Several of Mary's family members are killed in the battle, and one of her daughters is shot through the abdomen. Mary's sister sees the death of her family members and asks God to let her die with them. As soon as she says this, she is struck down by a bullet. The Indians surround Mary and tell her they will spare her life is she comes with them. Carrying her wounded daughter, Mary is whisked away into the wilderness by the Indians.

As they travel through the woods, one Indian allows Mary and her daughter to ride upon his horse, but they are so weak that they tumble from the horse's back. Another Indian, hearing the constant moaning of Mary's daughter, offers to kill the girl for her. Mary's Indian captors reach their woodland settlement, and Mary is given as a slave to an Indian leader named Quannopin. Soon afterward Mary's daughter dies, and the Indians bury the girl without her knowledge.

Mary's life as a slave is unpleasant as Wettimore, the wife of Quannopin, is cruel to her. Once she threatens to kill her with a stick of firewood if Mary does not hand over her apron. Mary meets another captured colonist, Robert Pepper, who tells her that her other captured children might be in the same Indian settlement and shows her some special leaves to put on her wound. Mary manages to briefly reunite with her older daughter and her son, who are also Indian captives. An Indian gives Mary a Bible, but Wettimore does not like Mary's constant reading of the scriptures.

Soon the Indians go on the move to avoid the English army, and they struggle to find food in the wilderness and are forced to eat unsavory foods, such as horse liver and old bones. Mary smuggles a piece of bear meat in her pocket, but it becomes rancid. During this process of marching and camping, Mary meets King Philip himself, who offers her a smoke on her pipe. Mary refuses since this is a bad habit she has previously overcome. Once while marching, King Philip himself helps Mary through a swamp. These details show that the Indians were not inhumane to their captives. The narrative ends when Mary is ransomed and allowed to return to her husband.

CONNECT

The Sovereignty and Goodness of God, Together with the Faithfulness of His Promises Displayed: Being a Narrative of the Captivity and Restoration of Mrs. Mary Rowlandson **by Mary Rowlandson** One of the most widely read prose works of the 17th century, Rowlandson's narrative captures the first-hand details of her captivity and offers her interpretation of these events as examples of God's goodness. Read excerpts from the original text and compare it to this script-story version.

ANTICIPATORY QUESTIONS

- Have you ever been around someone with a lifestyle vastly different than your own?
- Do you think the European settlers and the American Indians stayed peaceful for very long? Explain.
- Does everything happen for a reason? Explain.

TEACHABLE TERMS

- **Captivity Narrative** Rowlandson's story was one of the earliest captivity narratives, wherein a person of European descent survives capture by natives. Captivity narratives were bestsellers in Europe, where readers were hungry for stories about the "savages" of the New World.
- **Theme** Throughout her harrowing story, Rowlandson stresses her belief that all things happen for a reason. In his classic work of psychology, *Man's Search for Meaning,* Dr. Viktor Frankl, a survivor of the Nazi concentration camps of World War II, tells how the best chance for survival in the camps was not physical endurance or general health but a sense that the experience, no matter how horrifying, had some ultimate meaning for the prisoner. Those who had strong religious faith, committed political views, or even just a strong love of family were far more likely to survive. Examine the ways that Rowlandson relies on her faith in times of hardship.

RECALL QUESTIONS

1. Who or what does Mary struggle to carry through the wilderness?
2. What is one kindness that the Indians offer Mary?
3. Who is Wettimore?
4. What bad habit did Mary give up?
5. What does Mary smuggle inside her pocket for a few days?

CAPTURED BY INDIANS

THE NARRATIVE OF MARY ROWLANDSON

CAST

ROWLANDSON	*Puritan Woman*
HUSBAND	*Husband of Rowlandson*
JOSEPH	*Son of Rowlandson*
MARY	*Daughter of Rowlandson*
SARAH	*Daughter of Rowlandson*
BROTHER-IN-LAW	*Husband of Sister*
SISTER	*Sister of Rowlandson*
YOUNG MAN	*Man of Lancaster*
WILLIAM	*Nephew of Rowlandson*
INDIAN ONE	*Enemy Indian*
INDIAN TWO	*Enemy Indian*
PEPPER	*Captured Englishman*
MOTHER	*Captured Englishwoman*
QUANNOPIN	*Indian Warrior*
WETTIMORE	*Wife of Quannopin*
PHILIP	*Indian Leader*

NARRATOR: Over fifty years had passed since the Pilgrims first made their treaty with the Wampanoag chief, Massasoit—setting a precedent of peace between the European colonists and the Native Americans. But times had changed. More and more European settlers flooded into the New World, and they did not respect the established peace. New colonies sprang up—encroaching upon the Native American territories.

Massasoit's son, Metacomet—known as "King Philip" by the English—was now the chief of the Wampanoag, and land sales to the English had forced their tribe into more confined spaces. Tensions between the colonists and the Indians increased, and then the long-held peace dissolved. King Philip led a coalition of Indian tribes in open war against the colonists. *(sounds of war)*

Mary Rowlandson lived in the settlement of Lancaster, Massachusetts. She was the thirty-eight-year-old Puritan mother of three children. Her husband was the town minister—one of Lancaster's most influential leaders. When Reverend Rowlandson heard word that King Philip and his Indian allies had begun attacking local settlements, he made a difficult decision.

HUSBAND: Mary, I must go to Boston and ask them to send reinforcements. Our little hamlet is not equipped to withstand King Philip and his allies.

ROWLANDSON: Go, husband. I will stay behind with our children and pray for your speedy return.

NARRATOR: Little did Reverend Rowlandson know that during his absence, a force of 1,500 Indian warriors would attack his unfortified town, and his family would be dragged away by enemy hands. Years later when Mary Rowlandson wrote the narrative of her captivity among the Indians, she recalled all these terrifying events.

ROWLANDSON: (*narrating*) I can remember a time when I used to sleep quietly through the night—without the constant working of my mind. But now it is otherwise. When all others are fast asleep around me, my thoughts are upon things past. I remember how not long ago I was in the midst of a thousand enemies with nothing but death around me.

NARRATOR: Aware that King Philip's army was on the move, the villagers of Lancaster had taken up residence in four of the most fortified houses. About sunrise on February 10th, 1675, Mary Rowlandson awoke to the sound of gunfire. (*sounds of gunfire*)

ROWLANDSON: (*gasping*) Children! Get up quickly! I hear gunfire! Warn the others to arm themselves!

NARRATOR: Thirty-seven of the other townspeople had been living in the Rowlandson home. Rowlandson looked out her window into the village street. Several houses were already burning. (*sounds of screaming and burning houses*)

ROWLANDSON: Lord, preserve us!

NARRATOR: Then she saw them—dark forms moving back and forth through the flames—Indians bearing stone hatchets and clubs. (*screams of fright*) They disappeared into one of the homes that was already ablaze and dragged the family out into the street—a man, his wife, and their baby. Using their clubs, the Indians quickly knocked them in the head one by one.

Running into the living quarters of the her home, Rowlandson saw that many of the family members and other townspeople gathered there were furiously loading their muskets—staring out the window in horror.

BROTHER-IN-LAW: Look!

NARRATOR: They saw a young man running for his life toward the Rowlandson house. (*gunshot*) Before he could make it, a bullet wounded him, and he fell to the ground.

YOUNG MAN: (*cry of pain*) Argh! No!

NARRATOR: An Indian, raising his flintlock musket in triumph, leapt from a nearby rooftop and drew his hatchet as he neared his victim.

YOUNG MAN: Please! No! I will give you anything! Money! Whatever you want.

NARRATOR: The Indian did not respond but instead brought his hatchet down upon the young man's head and then expertly disemboweled him.

Rowlandson's brother-in-law, having finally loaded his musket, raised it to the window to fire, but a sudden spray of bullets hit the side of the house like hail. (*spray of bullets*) The brother-in-law fell back—holding a bullet wound in his neck.

BROTHER-IN-LAW: (*coughing*) They have us surrounded. We need to get out of here as soon as possible.

ROWLANDSON: Lord, what shall we do?

NARRATOR: Those within the Rowlandson house watched helplessly as they saw more and more of the villagers flee their homes—only to be butchered by the Indians. (*Indian war cry*)

ROWLANDSON: *(narrating)* It was a solemn sight to see so many Christians lying in their blood—like a company of sheep torn by wolves.

NARRATOR: The men within the house did their best to hold off the attackers, firing their muskets out the windows, but the Indians had hidden themselves on the nearby rooftops—making them difficult targets. Then they heard a noise that caused their hearts to freeze—footsteps upon their own roof. *(footsteps on the roof)*

BROTHER-IN-LAW: *(to his son)* William, run to the other side of the house! See what is going on there!

NARRATOR: The boy ran and returned white-faced.

WILLIAM: They have taken flax and hemp from the barn and laid it against that side of the house. Now they are setting it alight.

ROWLANDSON: *(narrating)* It was a dreadful hour. Some in our house were fighting for their lives. Others were wallowing in their blood. The house was on fire over our heads, and the bloody heathens outside were ready to knock us on the head if we stirred out.

NARRATOR: At last Rowlandson decided it was time to flee.

ROWLANDSON: If we do not run, we will die! I will lead the children out.

NARRATOR: Rowlandson turned to her fourteen-year-old son, Joseph.

ROWLANDSON: Joseph, you must help me! Be brave, my boy.

NARRATOR: Rowlandson's sister stepped forward.

SISTER: Sister, take my children as well.

NARRATOR: Rowlandson gathered up her children—Joseph, Mary, and Sarah—and some of her sister's children. She nodded to the house's defenders to throw open the door. Keeping the children in a tight bundle about her, she hurried out the door. *(loud gunfire)* As she ran across the threshold, the gunfire was so thick it was like someone had slung handfuls of rock against the house.

ROWLANDSON: *(shrieking)* Back to the house!

NARRATOR: Shielding the children, Rowlandson fell back across the threshold as they slammed the door behind her. Fortunately, no one had been wounded.

ROWLANDSON: We must all go at once, and you with the muskets must defend us.

SISTER: Leave the protection of the house?

ROWLANDSON: The house is ablaze! If we do not leave, we will all perish.

BROTHER-IN-LAW: William and I will go with you.

SISTER: *(fearfully)* I—I—cannot.

BROTHER-IN-LAW: Then stay here with the other children, and we will come back for you once Mary is away.

NARRATOR: Rowlandson gathered up her six-year-old daughter, Sarah, in her arms, and the group made ready to flee. Her brother-in-law flung open the door, and in a group they ran. As the Indian's gunfire filled the air,

Rowlandson's brother-in-law aimed his own musket toward his enemies. *(gunshots)* A bullet caught him in the chest, and he fell to the ground. The Indians hallooed a victory shout and were upon him—stripping him of his clothes. *(sounds of a scuffle)* Young William stopped to stare in horror at the death of his father.

ROWLANDSON: Run, William!

NARRATOR: Another bullet split the air, shattering William's leg, and he fell to the ground. In an instant an Indian was upon him—clubbing him in the head and ending his life.

In spite of the horror all around Rowlandson continued to run. *(gunshot)* Suddenly she felt a bullet pierce her side.

ROWLANDSON: *(cry of pain)*

NARRATOR: She fell to the ground.

JOSEPH: Mother!

NARRATOR: A group of Indians swarmed Rowlandson and her bloody bundle of children.

ROWLANDSON: Please! Spare my children! Please!

NARRATOR: The Indians lowered their deadly hatchets and seized the Rowlandson children up to inspect them.

Across the street Rowlandson saw her sister standing in the threshold of the house—flames blazing around her. She was weeping at the sight of her husband and son murdered before her eyes.

SISTER: *(crying out)* Lord, let me die with them!

NARRATOR: No sooner had she uttered these words than an Indian's bullet struck her down, and she fell dead over the threshold.

The other defenders of Rowlandson's home were apprehended by the Indians. One man, who had been chopped in the head, was crawling about in the street. Mothers were dragged one way, and children the other way. It was as if hell had come to earth.

After the Indians had inspected the Rowlandson children, they began to drag them away in opposite directions.

ROWLANDSON: No! No!

MARY: *(weeping)* Mother! Help!

NARRATOR: Rowlandson was helpless as her children, Joseph and Mary, were dragged away, but she still clung viciously to the weeping Sarah in her arms. It was only then that Rowlandson noticed why Sarah wept. The bullet that had pierced her own side had gone through the bowels of Sarah as well.

ROWLANDSON: Oh Lord, please preserve us.

NARRATOR: The Indian that held Rowlandson's arm stared at her menacingly—his hatchet still dripping blood.

INDIAN ONE: Come away with us. You will not be harmed.

ROWLANDSON: *(narrating)* I had always vowed—if ever attacked by Indians—I would rather die than be taken captive by them. Yet now the sight of their glittering weapons daunted my spirit, and I nodded my consent.

NARRATOR: Seizing up their captives, the Indian attackers let out a cry of victory.

(Indian cry of victory) Then they whisked their captives away into the dark woods.

ROWLANDSON: *(angrily)* You may have taken our village, but my husband will come for me.

INDIAN ONE: Then we will kill him as well.

NARRATOR: As her captors led her into the wilderness, Rowlandson entered a world that many colonists had only dreamed of in their worst nightmares. Rowlandson later wrote of her feelings during these events.

ROWLANDSON: *(narrating)* My pen cannot express the sorrows of my heart and the bitterness of my spirit. But even in such a place God was with me, carrying me along and bearing up my spirit so that it did not quite fail.

NARRATOR: On a hill not far from Lancaster the Indians made camp and built an enormous bonfire to celebrate their victory. *(sounds of a celebration)*

ROWLANDSON: *(narrating)* Oh, the roaring and singing and dancing and yelling of those black creatures in the night. It made the place a lively resemblance of hell.

NARRATOR: The next morning, Rowlandson's captors rousted her from sleep and forced her to march on through the woods. Her wound had begun to fester, and it was extremely painful for her to carry Sarah any longer. One Indian allowed the little girl to ride upon his horse. But when Rowlandson placed her daughter upon the horse, Sarah only began to whimper more loudly.

SARAH: *(whimpering in pain)* I shall die. Mother, shall I die?

ROWLANDSON: Shhh, my dear. Shhhh.

NARRATOR: There was nothing Rowlandson could do to ease the suffering of her daughter. As the Indians drove them on deeper in the forest, she carried Sarah in her arms although it caused her to almost faint from exhaustion. At last she staggered and fell to the ground.

INDIAN ONE: Here. You both ride.

NARRATOR: The Indian placed Rowlandson and her daughter upon the horse, but soon after, when descending a steep bank, Rowlandson and Sarah, both weak and weary, tumbled from its back. *(laughter from the Indians)*

ROWLANDSON: *(narrating)* The cruel savages mocked us with their laughter.

NARRATOR: It began to snow, and their misery increased. After hours of travel they camped for the night. Rowlandson cradled her wounded daughter in her lap.

SARAH: *(weakly)* Mother, I am thirsty.

ROWLANDSON: Shhh.

NARRATOR: Rowlandson felt that Sarah now had a fever, and her own wound was so stiff and hurting that she could barely sit upon the ground.

ROWLANDSON: *(narrating)* It was the Lord's mercy that my soul did not sink under such affliction.

SARAH: *(moaning)*

NARRATOR: That night Sarah moaned in constant suffering. Upon many occasions, an

Indian came to Rowlandson and offered to put the child to death.

INDIAN ONE: I will knock your child in the head for you—if you wish.

ROWLANDSON: You are as miserable comforters as those of Job.

NARRATOR: The forced march continued for several days, and Sarah grew worse and worse. At last they reached a huge Indian encampment. Over two thousand Indians—men, woman, and children—were gathered there, and many wigwams were spread out over the camp. Rowlandson noticed many of the Indians wore items of clothing that they had taken from English victims.

INDIAN ONE: You belong to Quannopin now. He is your new master.

NARRATOR: The Indians hauled Rowlandson and her daughter away and placed them in one of the wigwams of her new master. That night Rowlandson's fortunes would reach an all-time low. As she cradled her wounded daughter in her arms, Sarah departed from the world.

ROWLANDSON: *(narrating)* I must tell you that before this time I could never stand to be in the same room as a dead person. Now it was just the opposite. There was no place I could have been other than by my dear child's side. I lay down beside her all through the night. It was only through the wonderful goodness of God that he gave me the strength to not end my own wretched life.

NARRATOR: In the morning Rowlandson's captors commanded that she report to her new master.

INDIAN TWO: Your child is dead. Now you work.

NARRATOR: She rose and began to lift Sarah's body in her arms.

INDIAN TWO: Leave the child here.

NARRATOR: She reluctantly agreed and went to meet her new master, an influential Indian named Quannopin. One of his wives was King Philip's sister, Wettimore.

QUANNOPIN: This is Wettimore—sister of Metacomet. She is your mistress now.

NARRATOR: Wettimore was a haughty woman, who tried to lord over Quannopin's other wives. Her hair was powdered and her face painted. Jewels and beads hung from her ears. Her work was the making of girdles of wampum and beads.

WETTIMORE: You will sew for us.

NARRATOR: It was humbling for Rowlandson, who had always been the mistress of her own household and a respected woman in the community, to become the servant of another.

ROWLANDSON: I shall do whatever you require of me. But I know that my husband will soon ransom me.

NARRATOR: At these words Quannopin smiled.

QUANNOPIN: Your husband is dead. I killed him myself. *(chuckling)*

NARRATOR: Unsure whether to believe the Indian's bold assertion or not, Rowlandson returned to her wigwam. When she did, she cried out in shock.

ROWLANDSON: *(cry of shock)* My daughter! Where have you placed my daughter?

INDIAN TWO: She is buried now.

NARRATOR: The Indians pointed to the high hill nearby, and Rowlandson ran frantically to it. The ground there had been freshly disturbed.

ROWLANDSON: So I must leave her body here in the wilderness. *(sigh)* Her body, yes, but I commit her spirit to God on high.

NARRATOR: Numbly Rowlandson returned to her wigwam.

ROWLANDSON: Two more children have I—out there somewhere in the wilderness. I will survive and see them again.

NARRATOR: One day as Rowlandson was going about her sewing work, her mistress came into the wigwam where she labored.

WETTIMORE: Give me your apron.

ROWLANDSON: I will not. It is mine.

NARRATOR: The squaw picked up a piece of firewood, big enough to beat Rowlandson to death, and advanced toward her.

WETTIMORE: Give me your apron!

NARRATOR: Wettimore swung the stick of firewood at Rowlandson with all her strength, but Rowlandson dodged to the side. *(crashing sound)* Rowlandson furiously undid her apron and flung it at her mistress.

ROWLANDSON: Here! Take it!

NARRATOR: Wettimore departed, satisfied with the apron.

ROWLANDSON: She is a proud and vain savage.

NARRATOR: As Rowlandson settled back into her work, she was startled to see a man's face appear in the entrance of her wigwam. It was the face of a fellow colonist, who introduced himself as Robert Pepper.

PEPPER: For the five months since I was captured in battle, I have lived here among the Indians. I know that they have captured you in hopes that your husband shall ransom you. They have many captives here in the camp.

ROWLANDSON: Do they? What about my children? Joseph is fourteen, and Mary is ten. Are there any children here about that age?

PEPPER: I believe so, and your master should let you visit them.

ROWLANDSON: Oh, heaven be praised!

PEPPER: But I would search for them quickly. The Indians are being pursued by the English army. The army has burned their crops, and they have very little to sustain themselves. They are growing desperate.

NARRATOR: As Rowlandson stood, the man saw that she was wounded. He drew some leaves that looked like the leaves of an oak from his bag and showed her how to apply them to her wound. These greatly eased Rowlandson's suffering.

ROWLANDSON: *(narrating)* As the Lord wounded me with one hand, so he healed me with the other.

NARRATOR: Rowlandson wandered from wigwam to wigwam in the huge Indian camp—searching for any sign of her children. At last she caught sight of her daughter, Mary—sitting just inside one of the doorways. When Mary saw her mother, she cried out.

MARY: *(weeping)* Mother! Mother!

NARRATOR: Rowlandson learned from her daughter that she had been traded from one Indian to another for a gun.

MARY: *(weeping)* Mother, take me from this place! Save me!

ROWLANDSON: I cannot, my dear.

NARRATOR: Mary wept so loudly and clung to her mother so desperately that Mary's Indian owner finally shooed Rowlandson away. The heartbreak was almost too much for Rowlandson to bear.

MARY: Mother! Don't leave me here! Please!

ROWLANDSON: *(narrating)* One child I had laid in the ground, and the other was there with me—lost in the wilderness. The third was I knew not where.

NARRATOR: As Rowlandson departed this meeting with her daughter, heartbroken and distraught, she cried out to God.

ROWLANDSON: Lord, please send me some sign of relief—some sign of hope.

NARRATOR: As she returned to her master's wigwam, she looked up to behold her son approaching her through the Indian camp.

ROWLANDSON: Joseph! Joseph!

JOSEPH: Mother!

NARRATOR: Joseph had been sent to an Indian camp some miles away. News of his mother being in this camp had reached him, and his master had released him to come to her. Rowlandson told Joseph that his sister Mary was in the same camp as well.

JOSEPH: But what about Sarah?

NARRATOR: Rowlandson's eyes filled with tears.

ROWLANDSON: She has gone to heaven, my son.

NARRATOR: Eventually Joseph was called upon to return to his own master, and mother and son were again parted.

Soon afterward a party of warriors arrived in the Indian camp—loudly celebrating a victory. *(shouts of victory)* With them they bore a fresh batch of Englishmen scalps, which they displayed proudly. A village called Medfield had fallen to a raid.

One of the Indian warriors saw Rowlandson watching them from her wigwam, and he came toward her. In his hand he was carrying a worn book. It was a Bible.

INDIAN TWO: Here.

ROWLANDSON: Thank you. Do you think my master would let me read it?

NARRATOR: The Indian nodded. Rowlandson considered it one of the greatest gifts she would ever receive. She pored over it day and night and found comfort from the Holy Scriptures.

Her mistress, Wettimore, however, was displeased by Rowlandson's constant reading.

WETTIMORE: Less reading! More work!

NARRATOR: On one cold evening when Rowlandson and her mistress sat before a fire sewing, Rowlandson adjusted the fire to allow herself some of the warmth, Wettimore flew into a rage and flung ashes into Rowlandson's eyes.

WETTIMORE: The fire is not for you!

NARRATOR: Fortunately, Rowlandson was not blinded, but her mistress continued to persecute her at every turn.

It happened that Rowlandson discovered several other colonists, who were held captive in the same camp—a group of children attended by a pregnant mother with a young child in her arms.

MOTHER: *(yelling)* Let me go, you brutes! Let me go!

NARRATOR: Rowlandson tried to comfort this woman as best she could.

MOTHER: I have been begging them to let me go. I am so near my time to deliver. I have even thought of escaping if they will not let me go.

ROWLANDSON: No! We are many miles from any English settlement. It would mean certain death for you.

NARRATOR: But the pregnant mother continued to make such a wailing fit of it.

MOTHER: Let me go, you savages! I must be released to give birth to my child!

NARRATOR: Finally, she so exasperated her Indian captors that they clubbed her and her child in the head and then threw them into a fire and burned them up. They made the other captive children watch this and then warned them never to ask to leave, or they would suffer the same fate.

Not long after this event, the Indians made ready to remove themselves from that huge encampment. The English army was advancing, and they had to flee. Two thousand men, women, and children packed up and prepared to outrun an army. Rowlandson marveled at how expertly the Indians were able to move from place to place.

ROWLANDSON: *(narrating)* They marched on furiously with their old and young. Some carried their old, decrepit mothers.

NARRATOR: The Indians' progress was halted, only temporarily, by a river, where they made rafts to float across.

ROWLANDSON: *(narrating)* I was fortunate that they placed me upon a raft, and I did not even get my foot wet.

NARRATOR: Upon the other side, they made camp. For sustenance the Indians had little to offer themselves—let alone their prisoners.

ROWLANDSON: *(narrating)* My mistress kept me in an almost constant state of starvation. Yet if I went about begging for food, she chided me. She was embarrassed for not feeding me better, I suppose.

NARRATOR: On this occasion Wettimore gave Rowlandson a broth made from a boiled horse leg.

ROWLANDSON: *(narrating)* My first week among the savages I nearly starved, but after that somehow I stomached the things that they offered me. I drank a horse-leg broth and drank it thankfully. For the hungry soul every bitter thing is sweet.

NARRATOR: As the Indians continued to flee, their rations grew scarcer.

ROWLANDSON: *(narrating)* Once I saw an Indian carrying a horse liver with him, and I told him to give me a bit of it.

INDIAN TWO: Can a white woman eat horse liver?

ROWLANDSON: *(narrating)* I showed him. I roasted it in the coals, and although it was still bloody in my mouth, I stomached it.

NARRATOR: But horse liver was not the most bizarre food that Rowlandson ate.

ROWLANDSON: *(narrating)* Once while I was out begging for food, a squaw gave me a piece of bear meat. I smuggled it around in my pocket—fearing my mistress would steal it from me if I showed it to her. But after some time the meat began to stink, so I snuck out to find the same squaw again, who let me boil it in her pot.

NARRATOR: Harried and driven on by the advancing army, Rowlandson's captors were barely better off than she.

ROWLANDSON: *(narrating)* It amazed me how God provided for my enemies in the midst of such a desolate wilderness. They would pick up old bones and cut them into pieces at the joints. If they were full of worms and maggots, they would scald them over the fire to make the vermin come out. Then they would boil them and drink the liquor. They would eat horse guts and ears—as well as all kinds of meat—bear, venison, beavers, tortoise, frogs, squirrels, dogs, skunks, rattlesnakes, and even the bark of the trees.

NARRATOR: It was during these harsh conditions that one of Wettimore's young children died.

ROWLANDSON: *(narrating)* Much like I had done with my own daughter, Wettimore was forced to lay her daughter in the ground.

NARRATOR: Upon returning from burying her child, Wettimore found Rowlandson seated in the wigwam, reading her Bible as she often did.

WETTIMORE: Hmph.

NARRATOR: The Indian snatched Rowlandson's Bible from her hands and hurled it out the door. Then she slapped Rowlandson roughly across the face. *(slapping sound)*

WETTIMORE: *(angrily)* Get out of my sight!

ROWLANDSON: *(narrating)* I did not understand Wettimore's cruelty toward me. Soon after though, I learned that her brother, King Philip, was in the camp and that he wished to speak to me.

QUANNOPIN: Metacomet—King Philip—will meet with you.

ROWLANDSON: Has my husband finally paid my ransom?

QUANNOPIN: Your husband has taken another wife. I heard the news today. *(chuckling)*

NARRATOR: A group of Indian warriors arrived at Rowlandson's wigwam to lead her to meet with their infamous leader. Although during this whole ordeal she had never once wept before her captors, she did so now.

ROWLANDSON: *(weeping)* Now I go to meet the brute, who will end my life.

INDIAN TWO: Woman, why do you weep?

ROWLANDON: Because you are going to kill me.

INDIAN TWO: You will not die.

NARRATOR: Rowlandson was led to a large wigwam on a hill—surrounded by warriors. She was shown inside, and there sat King Philip. The sachem or chief nodded politely to her and offered her a smoke upon his pipe, which she declined.

PHILIP: Will you not smoke?

ROWLANDSON: In the days before this misadventure, I used to have two or three pipes a day. But it was a wicked habit. I thank God that he has given me power over it.

PHILIP: Hmmm. Suit yourself.

ROWLANDSON: What will be done with me? Will I be released?

PHILIP: No.

ROWLANDSON: Then why have you brought me here?

PHILIP: Make a shirt for my son.

NARRATOR: King Philip gave Rowlandson a thick pancake made from wheat. She could not remember a more pleasant meal. So Rowlandson made a shirt for Philip's son, and the chief paid her a shilling for her services.

ROWLANDSON: *(narrating)* With the money I purchased a bit of horse flesh. It was money well spent. Later I found out that some of King Philip's allies were pressuring him to release me, but he had refused. So a captive I remained.

NARRATOR: The Indians continued traveling through the wilderness—meeting and mixing with other groups. But never once did Rowlandson see her son or daughter among any of the Indians. Once she gathered the courage to ask her master for news of them.

ROWLANDSON: What about my children? Are they still among your people?

QUANNOPIN: Your son—I have some news about him.

ROWLANDSON: You do? Please tell me!

QUANNOPIN: He was troublesome. So they killed him and cooked him.

ROWLANDSON: You lie!

QUANNOPIN: No lie. I ate a bit of him. Very tasty. *(chuckling)*

NARRATOR: The Indians finally made their way into a thick swamp—a place they hoped the English army could not follow. As Rowlandson slogged through the thick mud and water, she found herself unable to go further. Suddenly, she felt a helping hand at her side. She turned. It was King Philip himself—assisting her through the mud.

PHILIP: Here. Push on. Two more weeks, and you will be a mistress again.

ROWLANDSON: Do you speak the truth?

PHILIP: I do.

NARRATOR: In the midst of the swamp the Indians set up camp. Philip summoned Rowlandson to his wigwam again.

PHILIP: When did you last have a washing?

ROWLANDON: Not in this month.

NARRATOR: Philip went to fetch water for her himself. He arranged for a looking glass to be brought and ordered one of his squaws to feed her a mess of meat and beans and ground-nut cake.

ROWLANDSON: *(narrating)* I was wonderfully revived by this favor he showed me.

NARRATOR: Two Praying Indians (or Christian converts), Tom and Peter, arrived in the camp. They had agreed to mediate between the English and King Philip for the release of the captives. When Rowlandson was allowed to speak to them, she clung to their hands and cried.

ROWLANDSON: Do you have word for me of my husband? Is he alive? Is he well?

NARRATOR: They told Rowlandson that terms for her release had been reached. The two Indians escorted her back to Boston to meet with her husband. As they traveled, they passed through the town of Lancaster—burned and desolate now.

ROWLANDSON: *(narrating)* It was a grim reminder to me that I was fortunate to be alive.

NARRATOR: Rowlandson was reunited with her husband. Her daughter and son were soon after freed from captivity as well. In spite of the horrors she had encountered, Rowlandson was thankful for the lessons they had taught her.

ROWLANDSON: *(narrating)* Oh, the wonderful power of God mine eyes have seen. The Lord has showed me the vanity of earthly comforts. He has also shown me not to be vexed by everyday difficulties. I have learned to look beyond present troubles because I remember a time when I would have given the world for my freedom. I have learned the sovereignty and goodness of God.

DISCUSSION QUESTIONS

1. What parts of Rowlandson's narrative are the most shocking or disturbing? Explain.
2. How does she present her captors—as savages or human beings? Explain.
3. Mary Rowlandson's narrative became America's first bestseller. Europeans found her account fascinating. What about the narrative would make it interesting to European readers?
4. What part does Rowlandson's faith play in her account?
5. Compare and contrast Rowlandson to her Indian mistress, Wettimore. How are they similar and different?
6. King Philip, making his last stand in the deep swamp, was fatally shot by a praying Indian named John Alderman. After his death, Philip's wife and nine-year-old son were captured and sold as slaves in Bermuda. Philip's head was mounted on a pike at the entrance to Fort

Plymouth, where it remained for more than two decades. His body was cut into quarters and hung in trees. Alderman was given Philip's right hand as a reward. What do you think of this treatment of Philip? Was it just? Explain.

THE JOURNEY OF OLAUDAH EQUIANO
TEACHER GUIDE

BACKGROUND

While many immigrants chose to come to the New World voluntarily, what about those who didn't? Between the seventeenth and nineteenth centuries, about ten million people were captured in Africa and shipped to North and South America and the West Indies as slaves.

Olaudah Equiano was a young African boy when he was pulled from the life he knew and forced into the nightmarish world of slavery. Transported to the West Indies and America aboard a slave ship, Equiano might just have well been sent to another planet since the white people's ways were so foreign to him. After buying his freedom, Equiano used the harrowing events of his life to bring attention to the evils of slavery. As the abolition movement gained momentum in England, Equiano wrote his autobiography to give ammunition to the cause.

In later years Equiano traveled the world, but he never again returned to the United States—choosing instead to settle in England, where he married an English woman named Susanna Cullen. Although he titled himself "the African" for the rest of his life, Equiano never fulfilled his dream of returning to his native land.

SUMMARY

Equiano's story begins in Nigeria when he is a young boy, the son of a chieftain of the Ibo people. As his mother tells him, Equiano's first name, Olaudah, means "fortunate one." Early in life, Equiano learns that slavery is prominent among many of the local tribes, including his own. He also learns about the Oye-Eboe, a tribe who captures and sells slaves to the other tribes.

Equiano has many thrilling childhood experiences—witnessing a battle between his tribe and another and even helping defend himself and his sister against an Oye-Eboe assailant who attempts to kidnap them.

When Equiano is in his early teens, Oye-Eboe kidnappers sneak into the village and abduct him and his sister from their home. Although Equiano tries to save his sister, they are separated from one another. The kidnappers sell Equiano to a distant tribe, where he is apprenticed to a blacksmith. Equiano plots a way to escape back to his own tribe, but before this can happen, he learns that he is too far from his home and the road is too dangerous for him to return home. The blacksmith sells Equiano, and he passes from one owner to another until he reaches the coast of Africa.

In a village there Equiano is briefly united with his sister before they are again separated. Equiano is taken to the sea, where he sees a ship for the first time. He is sold to white slavetraders, who he believes to be evil spirits that will eat him. Equiano describes the filthy conditions of a slave ship: Hundreds of men, women, and children crammed into a tight space. He compares it to the world of the dead. Equiano refuses to eat, and for this he is beaten. Equiano witnesses a pair of slaves chained together, who decide to leap into the sea and drown rather than face life aboard the ship.

When the ship reaches Barbados, the slaves are auctioned off like animals. Equiano is shocked by his first sight of two-story buildings and horses and firmly believes he has been transported to a magical land. Equiano is sold to work on a plantation in Virginia. There he sees a slave woman who is forced to wear a muzzle over her mouth like a dog. After this Equiano is sold to a ship's captain and has many adventures sailing around the world. Eventually, he is able to buy his freedom. In the end Equiano says that he was indeed fortunate, and his life measured up to the meaning of his name.

CONNECT

The Interesting Narrative of the Life of Olaudah Equiano, or Gustavus Vassa, the African **(1789)** Equiano's autobiography is considered to be the first great slave narrative. His story struck a chord with abolitionists in both America and England. Many proponents of slavery considered slaves to be subhuman, but Equiano's eloquent narrative silenced this argument by showcasing the human dignity in his struggle for freedom.

ANTICIPATORY QUESTIONS

- Can you imagine being taken away from your home and family?
- What is evil about slavery?

TEACHABLE TERMS

- **The Middle Passage** The route that Equiano's slavemasters use to transport slaves from Africa to the New World is called the Middle Passage, a deadly journey infamous for its high mortality rate. According to some sources, as many as fifteen percent of the slaves transported by this route died.
- **Slave Narrative** Equiano's autobiography is one of the first published slave narratives. These firsthand accounts of slavery were used to further the cause to abolish slavery. Another later example is the autobiography of Frederick Douglass.
- **Author's Purpose** Although one of Equiano's goals is to tell the story of his life, his primary purpose is to expose the horrors of slavery to a public that was unwilling to confront these realities. Examine where or not you think he was effective in showing the evils of slavery.
- **Irony** Compare the meaning of Equiano's first name to the events that transpired in his life. Examine whether or not you think this contrast is ironic.
- **Culture** Equiano takes great pains to describe the culture of the Ibo people. Compare and contrast this culture with your own.

RECALL QUESTIONS

1. What is the meaning of Equiano's first name?
2. What person is abducted along with Equiano?
3. Who or what does Equiano believe to be evil spirits?
4. What horrifying place did Equiano think was the world of the dead?
5. What are two sights in the New World that make Equiano think he has entered a magical world?

THE JOURNEY OF OLAUDAH EQUIANO

ADAPTED FROM HIS AUTOBIOGRAPHY

CAST

EQUIANO	*Young African Boy*
FATHER	*Equiano's Father*
MOTHER	*Equiano's Mother*
SISTER	*Equiano's Sister*
TRADER	*Slave Dealer*
KIDNAPPER	*Abductor*
BLACKSMITH	*Metalworker*
WIFE	*Blacksmith's Wife*
SLAVEWOMAN	*Slave to the Blacksmith*
SLAVEMASTER	*White Slavemaster*
SLAVE	*Enslaved African*

EQUIANO: (*narrating*) I am Olaudah Equiano—the African. To introduce myself to you, I must first give you an account of the manners and customs of my home country. It has been decades since I have seen it, but all the adversity I have experienced in my life has only riveted the memories of my homeland into my mind. Whether the love of one's country is real or imaginary, I still look back with pleasure on the first scenes of my life. Although I will admit, it is a pleasure that has been mingled with sorrow.

NARRATOR: Equiano grew up in a region of Africa now known as Nigeria around the year 1745. Equiano's father was one of the elders or chiefs of his nation—the Ibo people. To signify his high rank, Equiano's father bore a mark upon his forehead.

EQUIANO: (*narrating*) This mark was achieved by cutting the skin across the top of the forehead and drawing it down to the eyebrows—to form a thick welt there. All the great leaders of the tribe had it, and I had seen the same mark conferred upon one of my brothers. I was just a boy, but I expected to wear that mark myself one day when I became a man. It was a great source of pride.

NARRATOR: Equiano's father was a powerfully-built man, whose only clothing was a long cloak wrapped loosely around his body. Men and women alike wore this type of garment. Almost every person wore cloth that was dyed a vivid blue—a color extracted from a berry brighter and richer than Equiano ever saw in Europe.

One day Equiano saw his father talking with some strange men. Their skin had a red tint to it that Equiano thought was odd. They were displaying some wares before him—firearms, gunpowder, hats, and dried fish—and his father was considering them.

FATHER: We have no need for these things.

TRADER: What about slaves?

NARRATOR: The trader nodded to a line of sorrowful-looking men behind him. Equiano saw nothing different about them—except that their hands were bound and their eyes were without hope.

FATHER: Where did you get these slaves?

NARRATOR: The trader smiled good-naturedly.

TRADER: Do not worry, friend. They are all criminals. They were sold to us by their own tribes. They will work hard for you.

FATHER: Hmph. Your words are false.

NARRATOR: Equiano noticed huge sacks among the traders' gear.

EQUIANO: *(narrating)* I did not understand the use of those large sacks until later in my life. It was my misfortune to discover their function.

FATHER: Move on.

TRADER: As you wish.

NARRATOR: The trader, still smiling, gathered up his wares and departed. As soon as they had gone, Equiano went to his father.

EQUIANO: Who were those men?

FATHER: They are Oye-Eboe. It means "red men living at a distance." I fear they are deceivers, and we must be wary of them. I suspect they stole those men from their homes and are selling them as slaves.

EQUIANO: Father, does such a thing happen?

FATHER: It does.

EQUIANO: But we have slaves. Where did we get them?

FATHER: They are prisoners of war from other tribes. Or thieves and adulterers from our own.

NARRATOR: Each master of a family had his own parcel of land—surrounded by a moat, a fence, or an earthen wall hardened like brick. Equiano's father was no different. In one room of the main hut Equiano's father slept with all his male children. In the adjacent room slept all of his father's wives—most men did not have more than two—and the female children. The habitation of the slaves was elsewhere.

EQUIANO: *(narrating)* In our nation the houses are built by driving stakes into the ground, crossing them with branches, and covering them inside and out with a plaster that contains cow dung to keep away the insects that would torment you by night. The roofs are thatched with reed.

NARRATOR: Equiano's father had a numerous family—in addition to many slaves—and Equiano had six siblings. Equiano was the youngest of the sons, and, of course, became the favorite of his mother. He was always with her, and she took great pains to form his mind.

MOTHER: Olaudah, in our people, every child's name has meaning. I named you Olaudah, which means "fortunate one." No matter what happens in this life, remember you are fortunate.

NARRATOR: In addition to many other things Equiano's mother taught him the religion of his people. One evening, she took him by the hand and led him to a strange part of the village where he had never been before.

MOTHER: Let me tell you about the unseen world. There is a great Creator in the sky, who made all things. He lives in the sun, and he is girt about with a great belt. He never eats or drinks, but…can you keep a secret?

NARRATOR: She leaned in closely to Equiano and smiled.

MOTHER: Some say he smokes a pipe. *(laugh)* This Creator governs all events—especially our deaths and our captivities.

NARRATOR: At the mention of captivity Equiano thought back to the slaves he had seen.

EQUIANO: Will I be taken captive? Will the Oye-Eboe come for me?

MOTHER: Not if we call upon the good dead to protect us.

NARRATOR: They had stopped before an abandoned hut. Equiano's mother had brought along a small portion of meat and a container of palm wine.

MOTHER: This is the tomb of my mother.

NARRATOR: She placed the portion of meat upon the ground and poured out a bit of her drink into the dust. Then she began to speak soft words. Eventually she began to cry and lament.

MOTHER: *(weeping and crying)*

NARRATOR: This continued for quite some time, and it grew dark. Equiano could hear mournful birds crying in the darkness, which mingled with the weeping of his mother. The whole scene chilled him to the bone.

EQUIANO: *(frightened)* Mother, let us go away from this place! The evil spirits will get us!

MOTHER: No! We must pray to our beloved dead! They will keep the evil spirits from carrying us away.

NARRATOR: Soon Equiano's mother ended her prayer, and the two returned back to their home through the gloom.

In war Equiano's people used bows and arrows, broad two-edged swords, and javelins. They also had shields that covered a man from head to toe. All of his people were taught the use of these weapons from an early age. Even the women were warriors and marched boldly out to fight along with the men.

MOTHER: Olaudah, you must learn the art of war. You must be quick and skillful—but also very smart, so you may outwit your enemies.

NARRATOR: So Equiano's mother trained him to be a warrior. His daily exercise was throwing javelins. His mother adorned him with emblems—as is the custom with his land's greatest warriors.

One night Equiano was asleep on his bed of animal skins—snuggled up against his mother, who always kept him nearby—when he heard a whimpering in the darkness. It was his sister.

Out of all his siblings, Equiano only had one sister, and being close to his age, she was very dear to him.

EQUIANO: What is the matter, sister?

NARRATOR: His sister was sitting up on her pallet—pointing into the corner of the hut. There, curled up into a heap, was a snake—full as thick as the calf of a man's leg and the color of a dolphin under the water. *(soft hissing)* Equiano rose from the bed and made toward the snake.

SISTER: No, Olaudah! You will be harmed!

EQUIANO: By this snake? No. It is a good omen. Mother says so.

NARRATOR: Equiano picked up the huge snake to show his sister it was quite harmless. It hung in his grip listlessly.

EQUIANO: See? You have nothing to fear with me around, sister!

NARRATOR: Equiano's mother had sat up in bed and was watching her son—holding the snake aloft. There was a proud smile upon her face.

MOTHER: This is a good sign, my son! You will be fortunate!

NARRATOR: It was not the only sign of Equiano's fortune. Not long after, the boy met a poisonous snake on the roadway, but the snake slithered right between his legs and paid him no heed. Equiano's mother, too, interpreted this as a sign of his future fortune.

EQUIANO: *(narrating)* I lived this happy, blissful existence until the age of eleven when an end was put to all my happiness. Agriculture was my people's chief employment. Everyone, even the children, engaged in it. But when we went to the fields, we took our weapons along. Enemy tribes would attack us in an effort to carry off people to sell to the traders. And it was here—in the fields—that I once witnessed a battle.

NARRATOR: The people of Equiano's village had been plowing in their fields when enemies—both men and women— sprang out of the underbrush on all sides. *(war cry of enemy tribe)*

MOTHER: Olaudah! Flee!

NARRATOR: As he fled, Equiano saw his mother unsheathe her broad-sword, and his father raise his mighty javelin. *(sounds of battle)* Equiano ran to a nearby tree and climbed into it. As he watched, his people obtained a victory. Many warriors of the enemy tribe were slain, and some were captured. The rest of them fled.

FATHER: Come down, son. All is safe now.

NARRATOR: Equiano's people went back to their village—singing a song of victory. *(songs of victory)*

EQUIANO: *(narrating)* My people were a nation of dancers, musicians, and poets. Every great event—such as a return from battle—was celebrated with a public dance.

NARRATOR: When the dancing was done, Equiano's people dealt with their prisoners. Among them was the chief of the enemy tribe. He offered Equiano's father an enormous ransom for his release, but Equiano's father refused and put him to death. A female warrior of note had been slain from the other tribe, and her arm was displayed in the marketplace, where the trophies were always exhibited. Some of the prisoners were ransomed back to their tribe, and the rest were kept as slaves.

EQUIANO: *(narrating)* There were slaves among my people, but how different their condition was than the slaves I came to know in the lands of the white men! With my people slaves do no more work than other members of the community, even their master. Their clothing and their lodging is the same as free people. The only difference is that they are not allowed to eat with those who are free-born.

NARRATOR: Although slavery was a common practice, there was something troubling about it to Equiano. He was haunted by images of those red-tinted traders with their menacing sacks.

After the attack by the enemy tribe, the adults of Equiano's people feared another, so they did not take the children to the field with them. They left some of the older children like Equiano to watch over the younger ones.

SISTER: Olaudah, why will you not play with us?

EQUIANO: Because I must watch for bad men, who might carry you away.

SISTER: I can protect myself! If they come here, I will yell at them! "May you rot!" or "May a beast take you!"

EQUIANO: *(laughs)* Ha! That is what you say to mean children when they pick on you. That will not work against a kidnapper.

NARRATOR: As the younger children began their games, Equiano climbed a tree to watch over them. His vigilance waned though, and his eyelids grew heavy. That is why he did not notice a dark form slink out of the underbrush and make for the children. A man, armed with a club and a giant sack, sprang into the midst of their game.

SISTER: *(cry of fright)* Ah!

EQUIANO: To arms! To arms!

NARRATOR: Some of the older children grabbed up their weapons while Equiano jumped from the treetrop—brandishing his own javelin. The kidnapper drew back at the sight of the armed children, and they surrounded him and pummeled him to the ground. *(cry of pain from the kidnapper)*

EQUIANO: One of you, go tell the adults what has happened! The rest of you, find some rope. We will tie up this villain.

NARRATOR: When the adults raced back to the village, they were shocked to see the kidnapper bound, and the children beaming proudly.

MOTHER: My Olaudah! You have done well, my boy!

FATHER: Yes, son. A fine job. Some day you will be the greatest warrior in the village.

NARRATOR: But it was not to be. A few weeks later when again the adults had gone into the fields, Equiano and his sister stayed behind to guard their homestead. Sitting together in their father's hut, they did not notice three forms crouching beside the doorway. Two wiry men and a woman sprang into the hut and grabbed them.

EQUIANO: Ah! Attackers!

SISTER: Olaudah!

NARRATOR: Equiano's spear was not near, or the struggle might have lasted longer. The two men grabbed Equiano and stuffed a gag into his mouth—while the woman did the same to his sister.

EQUIANO: *(muffled yelling)*

KIDNAPPER: Now, let's get them out of here!

NARRATOR: The two men carried Equiano between them—over the wall of their village and into the underbrush. When they were well into the foliage, they stopped and tied the children's hands and feet.

KIDNAPPER: There will be no wriggling out of that.

NARRATOR: It was then that Equiano noticed the reddish tint of his kidnappers' skin—Oye-Eboe. The kidnappers carried them on until darkness fell. Then they ungagged the children's mouths and commanded them to eat, but Equiano and his sister were so overcome with grief that they refused.

SISTER: *(crying)* I want my mother!

KIDNAPPER: Shut your mouth, you stupid girl! Do you want every beast in the wild to hear us?

NARRATOR: The next day they carried the children on further through the woods and finally braved the open road. There, to avoid suspicion, they unbound the children and commanded them to walk alongside them like normal travelers.

KIDNAPPER: Do not dare breathe a word, or we will kill you!

EQUIANO: Ha! You want us for money. If you kill us, all your effort will be wasted.

KIDNAPPER: Yes, but it would bring me great satisfaction to kill an insolent pup like you!

NARRATOR: When they finally saw other travelers on the road, Equiano cried out.

EQUIANO: *(yelling)* Help us! Help us please! We have been kidnapped.

NARRATOR: But the people only turned their heads and hurried on. Then the kidnappers bound Equiano, gagged his mouth, and stuffed him into a giant sack. The rest of that day was spent in darkness.

Finally, the bag was opened, and Equiano was dumped out upon the ground. His sister was there weeping, and he wrapped her in his arms. The kidnappers threw some food at their feet.

KIDNAPPER: Now eat.

EQUIANO: Never! My father is a mighty chieftain! And my mother is a valiant warrior! They will find us!

(laughter from the kidnappers)

KIDNAPPER: I've taken hundreds of children like you. Your parents will never find you. They will forget you soon enough.

NARRATOR: The only comfort Equiano and his sister had that night was being in each other's arms—bathing each other with their tears.

EQUIANO: *(narrating)* But alas! We were soon deprived of even the small comfort of weeping together. The next day proved a day of greater sorrow than I had yet experienced.

NARRATOR: The children awoke with a start. The kidnappers were prying them loose from each other's arms. They grasped frantically at one another.

SISTER: *(screaming)* Olaudah! Don't let them take me!

EQUIANO: Sister! Sister!

NARRATOR: But as Equiano struggled against them, one of the kidnappers brought his club down hard upon his head, and his grip faltered. Equiano watched helplessly as another kidnapper dragged his sister away—wailing and weeping uncontrollably.

EQUIANO: *(weakly)* No. No.

NARRATOR: Now Equiano was truly lost. Several days passed. They traveled on. When Equiano refused to eat, the kidnappers took to stuffing food into his mouth—forcing him to swallow.

At last the kidnappers dragged Equiano into a village. Its people were similar to his, and they spoke a similar language, but their dress looked different. A strong-looking man emerged from a forge, and the kidnapper shoved Equiano before him.

BLACKSMITH: Where did you get this slave?

KIDNAPPER: He was sold to us—a criminal in his own tribe.

BLACKSMITH: A boy?

KIDNAPPER: He is strong and healthy. He will serve you well.

NARRATOR: The blacksmith looked Equiano over and then nodded.

EQUIANO: *(narrating)* And so for the first time, I became the slave of another.

NARRATOR: Equiano's new master was a blacksmith—with a family of his own. They all treated Equiano extremely well and comforted him over the loss of his family. The master's wife was particularly kind to him—almost like a mother.

WIFE: Poor boy. I know you miss your family, but this is your home now.

EQUIANO: *(narrating)* My principal employment was working my master's bellows—a leather-covered pump with a handle—to keep the fires hot. I believe it was gold he worked, for it was of a lovely bright yellow color and was worn by the women of his people on their wrists and ankles.

NARRATOR: Equiano lived among the people there—becoming friends with the other villagers his age. It was a life that resembled his old life, but he could never eat with the others, for he was not free-born. His master allowed Equiano to accompany the village children wherever they went.

EQUIANO: *(narrating)* It was during this time that a plan for escape entered my mind. I had marked the location of the sun as I was led away from my home by the kidnappers. I knew my father's land lay toward the rising of the sun. So I resolved to run away the first chance I could.

NARRATOR: Yet another misfortune soon struck. One day as he tended the chickens, Equiano slung a rock at one of them. *(dying of a chicken)* An old slave woman saw this happen and began to yell at Equiano.

SLAVEWOMAN: (*old woman voice*) You'll pay for that! The master will flog you for sure, you little brat! Mark my words!

NARRATOR: Fearing a flogging, Equiano fled into the nearby woods. He would have run farther, but he had hoped to pilfer some food before a serious escape was made. Frozen with fear, he watched as the alarm was raised.

BLACKSMITH: Search the woods for him! He couldn't have gone far!

NARRATOR: Yet Equiano had concealed himself well, and the search continued until almost dark. He could hear the searchers speaking to one another in the darkness.

WIFE: I hope the poor boy has not tried to return to his home. If he did, he would surely die. His home is miles away.

BLACKSMITH: I know. And the wild beasts would get him for sure—if the slavetraders didn't first. Let us hope he is still near—for his sake.

NARRATOR: It was then that hope died in Equiano's heart. He knew it was too far and too treacherous to ever make it back to his home.

EQUIANO: (*narrating*) I abandoned myself to despair. My hope of home was lost. I was anxious for death to relieve me of all of my pains.

NARARTOR: The next morning, the old slavewoman found Equiano's body lying in the ashes of the previous night's fire. She poked him to make sure he was still alive.

SLAVEWOMAN: Master! Master!

NARRATOR: Shortly after this Equiano was sold to another family in another village then sold again. Each time it was to masters who resembled his own people. Their language was similar enough to his own for him to learn it. Slowly, as he worked his way closer and closer to the coast of Africa, he became accustomed to the life of a slave.

EQUIANO: (*narrating*) If I can say one thing to the credit of those sable destroyers of human rights, they were never cruel to their slaves. They would only bind us to keep us from running away. It was only later when I knew the white slavemasters, that I knew true cruelty from a master.

NARRATOR: Equiano had been sold once again. But this time, when he was led into a foreign village to be introduced to his new master, a miraculous sight greeted his eyes— a familiar face.

SISTER: Olaudah! Is that you?

NARRATOR: Equiano could hardly believe it! It was his sister! She gave a loud shriek and ran into his arms.

EQUIANO: (*narrating*) I was quite overpowered. Neither of us could speak. All we could do is weep. This reunion between me and my sister affected my new master. That night he allowed us to sleep in the same room—although he did lie down between us to make sure we did not run away. It was no matter though. We reached our arms across him and clung to one another all night— happy to be together again.

NARRATOR: But the fatal morning came, and Equiano and his sister were torn apart once again. She was to be sold, and the two young people wept as they were separated.

EQUIANO: *(narrating)* I was now more miserable, if possible, than before. All I could think of was her suffering. What if it was greater than mine? I would have gladly taken her suffering upon me if I could have.

NARRATOR: Never again did Equiano see his sister.

EQUIANO: *(narrating)* My dear sister, your image has been ever riveted in my heart. Did you die at the hands of an African trader? Did you find your way into the pestilence of a slave ship? Did your youth and delicacy fall victim to the lash and lust of a cruel overseer? I will never know—and it haunts me still.

NARRATOR: Equiano was sold again and at last reached the sea. The first object which saluted his eyes when he arrived there was a slave ship, riding at anchor and waiting for its cargo.

EQUIANO: *(narrating)* The sight of this ship—the like of which I had never seen—filled me with astonishment. But this was soon converted into terror when I was carried on board.

NARRATOR: Strange creatures came forward—men with white faces and long hair. At the sight of them Equiano shivered in fear.

EQUIANO: *(terrified)* These are the bad spirits my mother warned me about all those years ago!

NARRATOR: The men spoke a language different than any Equiano had ever heard. They hauled him aboard their ship, where he saw a large furnace burning. All around him was a multitude of black people of every description—men, women, and children—chained together with every one of their countenances expressing misery and sorrow.

EQUIANO: *(narrating)* I no longer doubted my fate. I had been taken into a world of evil spirits. These white men were even worse than the red men I had often feared. They were demons from another world.

NARRATOR: Overcome with anguish and fear, Equiano fell motionless on the deck and fainted.

When the boy awoke, the black traders who had brought him to the ship were standing over him.

TRADER: Wake up, boy. We don't get our money if you die.

EQUIANO: Please! Don't leave me here! Will those white creatures eat me?

TRADER: No. They will do much worse than that! *(laughing)*

NARRATOR: They just laughed and walked away—pocketing their money. One of the white men came forward and held Equiano's jaw and forced a strange liquid down this throat.

SLAVEMASTER: Here! This will make you feel better!

EQUIANO: *(choking)*

NARRATOR: He had never tasted liquor before, and it burned his throat.

SLAVEMASTER: Now settle down.

NARRATOR: The white slavemasters laughed as Equiano wretched at the liquor.

SLAVEMASTER: Now, let's get this shipment on its way!

NARRATOR: Equiano was herded in with the other slaves. As the sailors began to raise the rigging and hoist the sail, he stared in terror and wonder. The white slavemasters hooted and laughed at how he gawked.

SLAVEMASTER: This one's fresh as a daisy! Ha!

EQUIANO: *(narrating)* That must have made them feel better to think of what a savage I was and how "civilized" they were. But let all haughty Europeans remember, they were once uncivilized, too. Did that make them worthy to be slaves?

NARRATOR: In despair Equiano watched helplessly as his homeland grew smaller and smaller in the distance and then finally disappeared over the water.

SLAVEMASTER: Now put this cargo below deck.

NARRATOR: Going below deck was like entering the world of the dead. In the moaning darkness, a loathsome stench oppressed Equiano's nostrils. The slaves were crowded into such tight spaces that they almost did not have enough room to turn over. Men, women, and children were all chained there to one another.

EQUIANO: *(narrating)* The atmosphere was like breathing a pestilence. Sweat filled the air. Many of the slaves were sick. Tubs were placed in the darkness for the waste, and often the children would fall into these and nearly drown. The chains galled you. The air suffocated you. The shrieks of the women and the groans of the dying rendered it a scene of horror almost inconceivable.

NARRATOR: Out of greed the slavetraders had forced too many slaves into too small a space. They knew many of them would die, but they would still make a profit. It was a price they were willing to pay.

Finally, among the other slaves, Equiano found some of his own nation, and he spoke to them across the darkness of the ship's hold.

EQUIANO: Where are these white demons taking us?

SLAVE: Back to their own country.

EQUIANO: They have a country? I thought maybe this horrible place was their home. How do they make it move across the water?

SLAVE: There is some magic in the cloths they hang on the ropes. Some spell in them makes the ship move. They are taking us back to their home—to work for them.

EQUIANO: Only work? I expected something worse. These creatures are so savage. I saw them beat one of their own men to death the other day and then fling him into the sea like a brute.

SLAVE: They *are* savages.

NARRATOR: The ship made its way across the Middle Passage of the Atlantic—a route from the coast of Africa to the West Indies. It was a trip that many of the slaves did not survive. Those that died were the lucky ones.

EQUIANO: *(narrating)* As the days passed, I wished for my last friend—death—to relieve me.

NARRATOR: When word reached the slavemasters that Equiano would not eat, they hauled him up on deck.

SLAVEMASTER: This one's not hungry, huh? We'll soon fix that.

NARRATOR: They laid Equiano across the windlass, one holding his hands and the other tying his feet, and then flogged him severely. *(sounds of a whipping)* Then they threw him, bloody and broken, back into the hold.

SLAVEMASTER: Now eat—or you'll be beaten again.

NARRATOR: From time to time, when the slaves would be hauled up on deck to be inspected, Equiano would stare at the sea. There was a netting over the side of the ship to catch things that fell overboard. Otherwise, he might have jumped and ended his life.

EQUIANO: *(narrating)* Some tried to end their lives in the sea. Any who tried to go over the netting were dragged back up and whipped. Any who did not eat were whipped.

NARRATOR: One day, when above deck, two slaves who were chained together leapt over the side of the ship and somehow made it through the netting. Equiano was standing nearby when this happened. The ship's crew was instantly alarmed. *(yelling of the slave traders)* Another old man, so ill and miserable, tried to jump overboard, but he only landed in the netting.

SLAVEMASTER: Stop the rest of them, or they'll all go!

NARRATOR: The slavemasters dragged the old man up and beat him within an inch of his life. The rest of the slaves were herded back below deck.

One day of the voyage, while above deck, Equiano saw fish leaping high up out the water. In spite of his misery, this sight thrilled him. Some of the flying fish leapt so far that they landed upon the deck of the ship.

EQUIANO: *(narrating)* How odd that men were leaping to their death from this vessel while these strange animals were leaping onto it and suffering the same fate. The sight of these flying fish only further convinced me I was in a magical world.

NARRATOR: The voyage continued, and within the hold the slaves were near the point of suffocation. This lack of fresh air and the stench of the waste tubs caused sickness to kill many of them. But at long last they reached their destination—the island of Barbados.

SLAVEMASTER: There it is, lads! Time to sell this cargo!

NARRATOR: Throughout the voyage the bodies of the dead slaves had been thrown overboard. Now the live ones were hauled to the deck—looking just as miserable. Many merchants came on board and examined the slaves attentively.

EQUIANO: *(narrating)* We were conducted immediately to the merchant's yard, where we were all pent up together like sheep in a fold without regard to sex or age. Slavery is a trade that treats men like animals. But isn't this the point? To depress the mind and extinguish every noble sentiment?

NARRATOR: As Equiano passed through his first New World city, he was shocked by all that he saw.

EQUIANO: *(narrating)* What struck me first was that the tall houses were built with stories, but I was still more astonished by seeing people on horseback.

NARRATOR: Then the slaves were sold in the usual manner. Families were auctioned off like beasts and separated from one another.

EQUIANO: *(narrator)* It is the mark of an accursed and wicked trade. Without scruple, relations and friends are separated, most of them never to see each other again. A group of brothers, who had been on the ship, were sold to separate masters. I heard them wail as they were parted.

NARRATOR: The sight of it made Equiano feel the pain of losing his dear sister all over again.

EQUIANO: *(narrating)* O, ye nominal Christians! Did you learn this from God? Did he not say, "Do unto others as you would have them do unto you"? Is it not enough to lose your homeland? To live a life of toil? Why are parents to lose their children, brothers their sisters, or husbands their wives? Surely this is a new refinement in cruelty.

NARRATOR: Equiano saw the many horrifying sights of slavery. From Barbados he was sold to masters bound for the British colonies in North America. There he lived on a plantation in Virginia.

EQUIANO: *(narrating)* Every new sight I saw added horror to the wretchedness that is slavery. On the Virginia plantation I saw a woman who had an iron cage placed over her mouth—like a dog—that restricted her speech and did not allow her to eat or drink. Her master did not wish her to bite.

NARRATOR: Each time Equiano was sold, he received a new name, to which he was forced to answer or he would be beaten. But deep down, he remembered his true name.

EQUIANO: *(narrating)* Here at this end of my life I see that my name did ring true. I have been fortunate. I was spared the hard plantation labor that put many of my countrymen into an early grave. Compared to their fate, I am a particular favorite of heaven.

NARRATOR: Finally, Equiano was sold to a ship's captain, who took him to sea. There he went on many adventures, and after years of success, he was able to purchase his own freedom in 1766. He continued to serve at sea for many years—sailing on expeditions to the Arctic and to Central America. He chose to make his home in England. Equiano's friends there taught him to read and to write and introduced him to Christianity, which was a great comfort to his wounded soul. He married a wife and raised a family. In the end Equiano became involved in the English abolitionist movement and wrote his autobiography to add to the cause. His story convinced many people to see the absolute evil of slavery.

EQUIANO: *(narrating)* My afflictions have brought me many miles. But I will still say I have been fortunate. I acknowledge God's mercy in every occurrence of my life.

DISCUSSION QUESTIONS

1. What is heroic and heartbreaking about Equiano's life? Explain.
2. What is horrifying about the slave trade?

3. Many proponents of slavery insisted that slaves were savages and did not have the same emotions and feelings or capacity for learning as "civilized" people did. How does Equiano's autobiography prove them wrong?
4. In fact, when Equiano's autobiography was published, many declared it to be a fake—claiming that a man of African descent could not write so eloquently. Why did they feel the need to view slaves as less-than-human?
5. Did Equiano finally have a happy ending? Explain.
6. Does slavery still exist in the world today? Explain.

THE SCARLET LETTER: PART I
TEACHER GUIDE

BACKGROUND

The Scarlet Letter is unquestioningly a pillar of American Literature (some argue the greatest American novel), but what does it have to offer young adult readers? Apart from peeling back layer after layer of symbolism, is there worth in making this novel required reading?

Sin, forgiveness, and redemption are timeless themes. Just like Hester Prynne, young people struggle with the consequences of bad choices. They, too, must accept responsibility for their actions without letting past mistakes determine their future. They must learn other important lessons: Morality is not determined by society and seeking revenge harms you more than it does your enemy.

It is a shame that many readers consider The Scarlet Letter to be a snooze. To alleviate this problem, this version of the text attempts to preserve the author's language and themes, yet make it more accessible to young readers, who still need to learn the lessons it has to offer.

Note: Reading questions and keys for each of The Scarlet Letter script-stories are available on the creativeenglishteacher.com website.

SUMMARY

After describing a wild rose bush that grows next to the rusted door of a Boston jailhouse, the story shifts to hundreds of years before when a crowd of curious townspeople have gathered before the same jailhouse door to see a prisoner, Hester Prynne, led out. The townspeople speculate on her punishment, and when Hester steps forth, carrying a baby in her arms, they see that there is a scarlet *A* embroidered on her bosom. Hester uses her baby to hide the letter from the crowd's view but realizes she cannot hide it completely. Although the townspeople expect Hester to look haggard from her prison stay, she looks luminous. The town beadle leads Hester to the pillory, where she must stand upon the scaffold as a public punishment. As Hester gazes into the crowd, she convulses with fear when she sees a gray-haired man whom she recognizes. The man is wearing a mixture of Indian and Puritan clothing and shows himself to be a stranger to the town when he asks the reason for Hester's punishment. The townspeople tell the stranger Hester's story: Her husband sent her across the sea from Europe to the New World ahead of him and then was apparently lost at sea. Now Hester has committed adultery with an unknown man, resulting in her child, and refuses to name the man. Her punishment is to wear the scarlet letter until her death as a badge of sin.

As the stranger watches, Reverend Wilson and young Reverend Dimmesdale ask Hester to confess the name of her lover, but she refuses, and the beadle returns her to the jail. In the jail Hester is visited by the stranger, who is actually her long lost husband. He has been living among the American native tribes, learning their ways, and from them has gained knowledge of herbal remedies. He gives Hester's baby a potion to quiet it although Hester fears it is poison. He also gives Hester a drink to calm her nerves. He assures Hester that he bears her no ill will, but he will assume the name of "Roger Chillingworth" and search for the identity of her lover. Out of fear of what Chillingworth might do, Hester promises to tell no one his true identity.

ESSENTIAL QUESTIONS

- How should we respond when others mistreat us?
- What is hypocrisy and why is it destructive?

CHARACTER ANALYSIS

Hester Prynne One of the great heroines of American Literature, Hester Prynne shows great fortitude in the face of persecution. She does not view her act of love as a sin, although it is condemned as such. The reader later learns why circumstances forced Hester and her lover to carry on their romance in secret. Hester defies the rules of society and teaches her fellow townspeople the true meaning of goodness. Bearing her persecutors no ill will, Hester symbolizes the power of forgiveness.

ANTICIPATORY QUESTIONS

- Who were the Puritans?
- What are some symbolic meanings of the color red?

SYMBOLISM

- **The Wild Rosebush** Growing next to the prison door on pg. 107, the wild rosebush is a symbol interpreted in many different ways. It can be a symbol of Hester herself, who will bloom in spite of adversity. It can also be a symbol of the goodness present in the darkness of human nature.
- **The Scarlet Letter** Probably one of the most famous symbols of all time, the scarlet *A* sewn onto Hester's clothing begins as a symbol of sin and shame. Further into the novel, the symbolism of the letter changes as Hester's actions cause the townspeople to look upon her positively.
- **Hester's Child** Pearl, Hester's baby with an unnamed father, is also a symbol of her sin and shame. On pg. 108 Hester attempts to hide the scarlet letter from the crowd by holding her newborn child over it, only to realize that one symbol of sin cannot hide another.
- **Chillingworth's Clothing** Wearing half "savage" clothing and half civilized clothing, Chillingworth, whose appearance in described on pg. 110, straddles two worlds. His knowledge of potions, which he learned in the wilderness, will help him in his diabolical mission.

RECALL QUESTIONS

1. What is embroidered on Hester Prynne's clothing?
2. According to the townspeople, where is Hester Prynne's husband?
3. What secret do the town ministers ask Hester to reveal?
4. What is strange about the way Roger Chillingworth is dressed?
5. What is the real identity of Roger Chillingworth?

THE SCARLET LETTER: PART I

CAST

WOMAN ONE	*Woman in the Crowd*
WOMAN TWO	*Woman in the Crowd*
WOMAN THREE	*Woman in the Crowd*
WOMAN FOUR	*Woman in the Crowd*
MAN ONE	*Respectable Man*
MAN TWO	*Respectable Man*
BEADLE	*Church Officer*
M. HIBBINS	*Old Crone*
HESTER	*Fallen Woman*
WILSON	*Colony Minister*
DIMMESDALE	*Local Minister*
CHILLINGWORTH	*Strange Man*
BRACKETT	*Jailer*

NARRATOR: If you happened to pass by the old prison house in the city of Boston, you would see that its oaken door hangs off its hinges, and its metalwork is now covered in rust. Yet on one side of the portal grows a wild rosebush, once offering consolation to those poor souls who were confined behind this barred door—or walked out of it again to their doom. Perhaps this rosebush symbolizes the sweet, moral blossom that can be found in the otherwise dark tale of human frailty and sorrow that has been associated with this prison house for generations.

On a summer's morning in the early seventeenth century, the grassy plot before this same jail was occupied by a large number of the inhabitants of Boston—all with their eyes fastened on the iron-clamped, oaken door of the prison. It was the type of crowd that gathered in anticipation of a public whipping or an execution. But today it was the women who were taking a peculiar interest in what was about to ensue.

WOMAN ONE: Goodwives, I'll tell you a piece of my mind! It would behoove our township if we mature women could handle the punishment of sinners like this Hester Prynne. What think you?

WOMAN TWO: I know if the hussy stood up for judgment before us women, she would not come off as easily as she has today!

WOMAN ONE: Of course not! The magistrates have gone easy on her, I say.

WOMAN THREE: *(kindly)* People say that Reverend Dimmesdale, our godly pastor, takes it grievously to heart that such a scandal should happen in his congregation.

WOMAN ONE: The magistrates are all God-fearing gentlemen. But I feel they have been over-merciful in this case. All they did was place a bit of fabric on her bodice.

WOMAN TWO: Her bodice? Ha! They should have taken a hot poker and branded her on her forehead!

WOMAN FOUR: The naughty baggage! Why would she care about a bit of cloth on her bodice? She could just cover it up with a brooch and walk around the streets as bold as ever.

WOMAN TWO: Just like none of this ever happened!

WOMAN THREE: *(tenderly)* She may cover the mark, but the pain will always be in her heart.

WOMAN FOUR: What do marks and brands matter to her? This woman has brought shame upon us all! The truth is, she ought to die. Is there no law to condemn her?

WOMAN TWO: Of course! Holy Scripture and the statute book of our colony.

WOMAN ONE: If they don't punish this woman to the full extent of the law, what do the magistrates expect to happen to their own wives and daughters? What will keep other women from going astray?

NARRATOR: A man, who stood nearby listening to the gossips, furrowed his brow.

MAN ONE: *(shocked)* Mercy, goodwife! Is there no virtue in woman—save what springs from a fear of the gallows?

WOMAN ONE: *(grumbling)* Death is a good antidote for sin among any of God's creatures.

NARRATOR: From out of nowhere, an old crone appeared in the crowd. It was Mistress Hibbins, the sister to the governor. The people pulled away from her as if touched by evil.

MISTRESS HIBBINS: *(cackling)* Death would be the easy way for her! This suffering and shame will bring her closer to the darkness…which will be most beneficial for some of us.

MAN ONE: Hush now, all you gossips! Here comes Mistress Prynne herself!

NARRATOR: The door of the jail was flung open, and the grim and grisly presence of the town beadle emerged, with his sword by his side and his staff of office in his hand. With his other hand, the beadle drew a young woman forward into the light. It was Hester Prynne. At the threshold of the prison, she shook off his hand and then stepped into the open air, as if by her own free will. *(murmuring in the crowd)*

WOMAN ONE: There is the child!

NARRATOR: Hester bore in her arms a baby of some three months old. The child blinked its eyes from the light of day. Until now it had only been acquainted with the gray twilight of a dungeon. *(wail of a child)*

WOMAN TWO: There is the mark!

NARRATOR: Elaborately embroidered upon Hester's bosom was a letter "A" in fine red cloth with gold thread. Now in the light of day it was Hester's impulse to clasp her child tightly to her bosom—not because of motherly affection, but to hide the token of shame that was fastened onto her dress. In a moment she realized that one token of shame would poorly serve to hide another, so she lowered her child, and with a haughty smile and an unabashed gaze looked around at her townspeople and neighbors.

WOMAN THREE: There doesn't seem to be a bit of shame about her!

NARRATOR: Never before had Hester Prynne seemed more ladylike than as she issued from the prison. She had dark and abundant hair, so glossy that it threw off the sunshine with a gleam. Those who had known her before had expected to behold her dimmed and obscured by a disastrous cloud. Instead they were startled to perceive how her beauty shone out and made a halo of her misfortune and ignominy. The scarlet letter, so fantastically embroidered and illuminated upon her bosom, had the effect of a spell, taking Hester out of the ordinary realm of humanity and enclosing her in a sphere by herself.

WOMAN THREE: One thing is sure—she has good skill with a needle.

WOMAN TWO: Ha! Apparently that is not the harlot's only skill!

WOMAN ONE: What a brazen hussy! The letter was meant for punishment, but she has pridefully embroidered it! She has practically decorated it!

WOMAN TWO: We should strip her rich gown off her dainty shoulders, along with that curiously-stitched letter! I'll give her an old rag from a sickbed to make herself a more fitting letter!

WOMAN THREE: Shhh! Do not let her hear you. I know that she felt every stitch of that embroidered letter in her heart.

BEADLE: Make way, good people! Make way in the king's name! In due time, Mistress Prynne shall be placed where man, woman, and child may have a good view of her shameful apparel. A blessing on the righteous colony of Massachusetts, where dark sin is dragged into the sunshine and exposed for all to see! Come, Mistress Hester! Show your scarlet letter in the marketplace!

NARRATOR: A lane opened through the crowd. Preceded by the beadle and attended by a procession of stern-browed men, scowling women, and curious schoolboys, Hester Prynne set forth toward the place appointed for her punishment—the town pillory in the marketplace, where offenders were whipped, placed in the stocks, and sometimes executed. *(murmuring from the crowd)*

It was no great distance from the prison door to the market place, yet it was a journey of some length for Hester. Every footstep of those who thronged to see her humiliation caused her agony, as if her heart had been flung into the street for them all to trample upon. Yet she sustained herself as best a woman might under the heavy weight of a thousand unrelenting eyes. At moments she felt as if she would shriek with the full power of her lungs and throw herself down upon the ground—or else go mad at once.

But, finally, the market place and the pillory scaffolding were reached. Hester and her child ascended the stairs for all the crowd to behold—like the Madonna, Mary, and her child.

BEADLE: Mistress Hester Prynne is sentenced to wear the emblem upon her bosom for all her life. Today she shall stand on this scaffold of the pillory for all to see her shame until the sun is high in the sky. Then she shall spend one more night in yonder prison. So is her punishment.

NARRATOR: Hester's child cried out, and she moved to comfort it. *(wailing child)* As Hester lifted her eyes from her child, at the back of the crowd, she noticed a strange, yet familiar, man. When she beheld him, she convulsed with such force that her poor child cried out in pain. *(wail of a child)*

The man's hair was graying, and one shoulder of his thin frame was higher than the other. His clothing was an odd mixture of civilized and savage heathen dress. As the stranger bent his eyes on Hester, a writhing horror twisted across his features like a gliding snake. His face darkened with some powerful emotion, which he instantaneously controlled by an effort of his will. He had noted that Hester had recognized him, so he slowly and calmly raised his thin finger and laid it upon his lips. Then the man touched the shoulder of a townsman who stood nearby.

CHILLINGWORTH: I pray you, good sir, I am a stranger here. Who is this woman and why is she publicly shamed?

MAN TWO: You must indeed be a stranger in this region, friend, if you have not heard of Hester Prynne and her evil doings. She has raised a great scandal! She has brought shame on Reverend Dimmesdale's church.

CHILLINGWORTH: Truly, I am a stranger. I have been a wanderer and met with grievous mishaps by sea and land. I have long been among the heathen savages to the south of here. Would you please tell me more of Hester Prynne?

MAN ONE: After your sojourn in the wilderness, it will gladden your heart to know you are in godly New England, a land where iniquity is searched out and punished in the sight of rulers and people.

MAN TWO: Yonder woman was the wife of a certain learned man, who was English by birth, but who had long dwelt in Amsterdam. Some time ago he decided to cross over and cast in his lot with us folks of Massachusetts. To this purpose he sent his wife across the sea before him, remaining behind himself to look after some necessary affairs.

MAN ONE: For two years that woman has been a dweller here in Boston, but no tidings have come of her husband. His young wife has been left to her own misguidance it would seem.

CHILLINGWORTH: If this man you speak of was so learned, he should have known that his wife would be up to some mischief without him. And who is the father of yonder baby that Mistress Prynne holds in her arms? It is some three or four months old, I would judge.

MAN ONE: In truth, friend, that matter remains a riddle. The one who shall expound it has yet to speak.

MAN TWO: Mistress Hester refuses to speak his name. The magistrates have tried to convince her to name the father, but it has all been in vain.

MAN ONE: The guilty one stands looking on at this sad spectacle. He is unknown of man and forgets that God sees him for what he really is.

CHILLINGWORTH: The woman's husband, this learned man, should come himself and look into the mystery.

MAN ONE: That would behoove him—if he still be alive.

MAN TWO: It is likely that her husband may be at the bottom of the sea, so they have not been bold enough to put her to the full extremity of the law.

MAN ONE: The penalty for her crime is death. But in their great mercy and tenderness of heart, they have doomed Mistress Prynne to stand as you see on the platform of the pillory. Then for the remainder of her natural life she will wear the mark of shame upon her bosom.

CHILLINGWORTH: A wise sentence! Thus, she will be a living sermon against sin—until the ignominious letter is engraved upon her tombstone! It irks me, nevertheless, that the partner of her iniquity should not stand on the scaffold by her side. But he will be known. *(aside)* Yes, he will be known.

NARRATOR: The odd man bowed to the gentlemen and took his leave. As he passed through the crowd, the man moved near the scaffold—never taking his eyes from Hester. Hester stared back at him with such a fixed gaze that she scarcely heard a voice behind her.

WILSON: Hearken to me, Hester Prynne!

NARRATOR: Hester turned her face toward the voice. Directly over the platform upon which she stood was a balcony extending from the church meetinghouse. Seated there was Reverend Wilson, the eldest clergyman of Boston, Governor Bellingham, and Reverend Master Dimmesdale, a young clergyman. Reverend Wilson stood tall with gray eyes and a border of grizzled locks beneath his skull cap.

WILSON: Hester Prynne, I have sought to persuade young Reverend Dimmesdale here that he should deal with you concerning the vileness and blackness of your sin! But he opposes me and says that it would be wrong to force a woman to lay open her heart's secrets in broad daylight. Reverend Dimmsedale, must it be you or I that shall deal with this poor sinner's soul?

NARRATOR: The crowd looked anxiously at Reverend Dimmsedale, who continued to hesitate. Although still young, his eloquence and religious fervor had given him high esteem among the people.

WILSON: Speak to the woman, my brother! Exhort her to confess the truth!

NARRATOR: Dimmesdale began to move forward—bending his head in a silent prayer. He turned his brown, melancholy eyes toward Hester Prynne.

DIMMESDALE: Hester Prynne, you hear what this good man says, and you see the accountability that I have to you and all my congregation. For the peace of your soul I charge you to speak out the name of your fellow sinner.

NARRATOR: The crowd waited in breathless anticipation.

DIMMESDALE: Be not silent from any mistaken pity and tenderness for this man! Believe me, Hester, even if he were to step down from some high place and stand there beside you on this pedestal of shame, it would be better for him than to hide a guilty heart throughout his life.

NARRATOR: Hester stood perfectly still—silent. Even her child did not make a sound.

WILSON: Defy us not, Hester Prynne! Pity for your plight has kept this sentence light. Push us not!

DIMMESDALE: What can your silence do for him? Heaven has granted you the earthly shame that will cleanse you from your sin. Although you have sorrow without, you have triumph over the evil within. Do not deny the same bitter but wholesome cup that is presented to your lips to this man, who may have not the courage to grasp it for himself.

NARRATOR: Every member of the crowd was moved by Dimmesdale's speech—even Hester Prynne's baby was affected by it. The babe turned its head toward him and held up its little arms with a pleased murmur. *(giggling of a child)* All the people were sure that Hester Prynne would speak out the guilty man's name.

WILSON: Will you speak?

NARRATOR: Hester shook her head.

WILSON: Woman, do not push your limits beyond Heaven's mercy! Your child there encourages you to speak as well. Speak out the name! This confession and your repentance may take the scarlet letter off your breast!

HESTER: Never! It is too deeply branded. You cannot take it off. I will endure *his* agony as well as mine.

NARRATOR: The strange man from the crowd suddenly cried out.

CHILLINGWORTH: Speak, woman! Speak and give your child a father!

NARRATOR: Hester stared at the man wildly.

HESTER: I will not speak! And my child must seek a heavenly Father, for she will never know an earthly one!

NARRATOR: Mistress Hibbins looked from Hester to the man in the crowd. She noticed the strange looks between them. She smiled and seemed to address the air around her.

MISTRESS HIBBINS: *(to herself)* What is this? There is a darkness here—between these two. I can see it. Perhaps they will strengthen our ranks at our dark meetings in the deep-forest night!

NARRATOR: Reverend Dimmesdale leaned back over the balcony with his hand on his heart.

DIMMESDALE: Wondrous strength and generosity of a woman's heart! She will not speak!

NARRATOR: Reverend Wilson began a long discourse on sin and used the scarlet letter as a symbol of the flames of the infernal pit. Yet Hester would not speak the name. She kept her place on the scaffold with glazed eyes and weary indifference. The crowd grew restless and disheartened. They returned home, still sure that the perpetrator was somewhere close among them.

Finally, Hester was led back to her prison cell. Some who followed behind and peeped into the dark hallway after her said that the scarlet letter threw off a lurid gleam in the darkness.

Imprisoned within her cell once again, Hester's child began to wail. *(wail of a child)* Hester laid it in its trundle-bed, ignored its cries, and beat her fists against the floor—beginning to sob and wail herself.

HESTER: *(weeping and wailing)*

NARRATOR: Her cries roused Master Bracket, the jailer.

BRACKETT: Mistress Hester! What is the meaning of these hysterics? If you do not stop, I shall be forced to call a doctor.

NARRATOR: But Hester did not stop her thrashing about, and Master Brackett began to fear she would do harm to herself or to the child. He ran out at once to find help and soon returned with a visitor.

BRACKETT: Look! I have returned! This good doctor has agreed to come. His name is Roger Chillingworth. Would you allow him to help you and your child?

NARRATOR: When Hester glanced up to behold the man's face, her weeping stopped. It was the stranger from the crowd. He smiled at her startled expression.

HESTER: I will not let him. I cannot. I pray you, be gone!

NARRATOR: Chillingworth turned kindly to the jailer.

CHILLINGWORTH: Prithee, friend. Leave me alone with my patients. Trust me, good jailer, I will calm the woman and her child. You shall have peace in your jailhouse. I promise you that Mistress Prynne shall hereafter listen to authority.

BRACKETT: Truthfully, she has been like one possessed. You will be a man of skill indeed if you are able to calm her. If not, I will have to drive Satan out of her with stripes from my whip!

NARRATOR: The jailer left Dr. Chillingworth alone with Hester. She did not take her eyes from the strange man.

CHILLINGWORTH: First, I shall attend to the child.

NARRATOR: Chillingworth made his way first to stare down at the child as it lay in its crib. As Hester watched him breathlessly, he examined the child and unclasped a leather bag from under his clothes. From it he poured a powdery substance into a cup of water.

CHILLINGWORTH: You know, for the past year I have traveled among the savages who taught me the kindly properties of herbs. Before that I studied the ancient art of alchemy. These two combined have made me a better physician than many that claim a medical degree.

NARRATOR: He held up the cup.

CHILLINGWORTH: Here, woman! The child is yours. She is not of mine. Neither will she recognize my voice. Therefore, administer this draught with your own hand.

NARRATOR: Hester did not reach out for the cup.

HESTER: Would you avenge yourself on my innocent child?

CHILLINGWORTH: Foolish woman! I would not harm this misbegotten and miserable babe. The medicine is potent for good. Were it my child—mine as well as yours—I could do no better for it.

NARRATOR: Hester still hesitated.

CHILLINGWORTH: I shall do it then.

NARRATOR: Chillingworth took up the child and administered the medicine to it himself. After a few moments the child's moans subsided into sleep. He set the child down in her crib and then turned to Hester.

CHILLINGWORTH: Now I shall examine you.

NARRATOR: He approached Hester, who stayed still—alert. He felt her pulse and looked into her eyes. His gaze made Hester's heart shrink and shudder. It was so familiar, but so strange and cold. He chuckled to himself and began to mix a second draught.

CHILLINGWORTH: I have learned many new secrets in the wilderness, and here is one of them.

NARRATOR: He held the drink out to Hester.

CHILLINGWORTH: Drink it! It may be less soothing than a sinless conscience. I cannot give you one of those. But it will calm the swell and heaving of your passion.

NARRATOR: Hester took the cup and stared at her child.

HESTER: I have thought of death. I have even wished for it. I would have even prayed for it—if it were fit for one such as I to pray for anything. Yet if death be in this cup, I ask you to think again before I drink. See! It is even at my lips.

CHILLINGWORTH: Drink then. Do you know me so little, Hester? Even if I concocted a scheme of vengeance, how could I do better than what you already suffer?

NARRATOR: He laid his long forefinger on the scarlet letter, which seemed to scorch into Hester's breast as if it had been red-hot.

CHILLINGWORTH: I would let you live so that this burning shame might still blaze upon your bosom. Therefore, live! And bear your doom with you! Your doom will be in the eyes of men and women—and in the eyes of yonder child. So that you may live, take of this draught.

NARRATOR: Hester drained the cup.

CHILLINGWORTH: Hester, I do not ask why or how you came to this disgrace. The reason is not far to seek. It was my folly and your weakness. I am a man of thought, a bookworm of great libraries—a man already in decay, having given my best years to feed the hungry dream of knowledge. What right did I have to link myself to youth and beauty like your own? From my birth hour I was misshapen. How could I delude myself into thinking I was wise? From the moment we descended the church steps as man and wife, I should have seen that scarlet letter blazing at the end of our path.

HESTER: You know I was frank with you. I felt no love for you, and I feigned none.

CHILLINGWORTH: True. That was my folly. I have said it. But up to that time in my life, I had lived in vain. The world had been so cheerless! My heart was a lonely and chilly habitation without a household fire. I drew you into my heart, into its innermost chamber, and tried to warm myself by the warmth you made there.

HESTER: I have greatly wronged you.

CHILLINGWORTH: We have wronged each other. Mine was the first wrong. It was when I tricked your budding youth into a false and unnatural relation with my decay. Therefore, I seek no vengeance, and I plot no evils against you. Between you and me, the scale hangs fairly balanced. But, Hester, the man lives who has wronged us both! Who is he?

HESTER: That you shall never know!

NARRATOR: Chillingworth smiled wickedly.

CHILLINGWORTH: Never, you say? Never know him! Believe me, Hester, there are few things in the outward world or in the invisible sphere of thought that can be hidden from the man who devotes himself to the solution of a mystery. You may cover up your secret from the prying eyes of the townspeople. You may conceal it from the ministers and magistrates. But not from me. I shall seek this man as I have sought truth in books—as I have sought gold in alchemy! I shall see him tremble! Sooner or later, he will be mine!

NARRATOR: The man's eyes glowed so intensely that Hester clasped her hands over her heart, fearing that he should read the secret there at once.

CHILLINGWORTH: He bears no letter of infamy sewed onto his garment as you do, but I shall read it on his heart. Yet fear not for him! Do not think I will interfere with Heaven's own method of retribution. I will not betray his identity and lose him to the grip of human law. No, that would be my own loss! Neither will I contrive against his life. Let him live! Let him hide himself! He shall be mine!

HESTER: (*frightened*) Your acts are like mercy, but your words show me that you are a terror—a demon!

CHILLINGWORTH: Listen. You, who were once my wife, I command one thing of you. As you keep the identity of your lover a secret, likewise keep mine. Breathe not to any human soul that you once called me husband. Whether by love or hate, right or wrong, your life, the life of your child, and the life of your love belong to me. So betray me not, Hester Prynne!

HESTER: Why do you desire power over our lives? Why not announce yourself openly and cast me off at once?

CHILLINGWORTH: Maybe because I do not want to encounter the dishonor that comes to the husband of a faithless wife. Maybe it is for other reasons. It is my intention to live and die unknown. Therefore, let your husband be to the world as one already dead.

HESTER: (*slowly*) I will keep your secret—as I have kept his.

CHILLINGWORTH: Good. Now recognize me not by word, by sign, or by look! Do not breathe my secret to even your lover. If you should fail me in this, beware! His fame, his position, his life will all be in *my* hands. Swear it!

NARRATOR: Hester swore it, and Chillingworth smiled a crooked grin.

HESTER: (*frightened*) Why do you smile so? Are you like the devil, the Black Man that haunts the forests around us? Have you tricked me into a bond that will prove the ruin of my soul?

CHILLINGWORTH: Not *your* soul. No, not yours. Now I leave you alone—with your infant—and your scarlet letter.

DISCUSSION QUESTIONS

1. Is the punishment of Hester Prynne merciful or cruel? Explain.
2. Based on this first episode, how does *The Scarlet Letter* portray the Puritans and their society?
3. The Puritans intended to create a perfect society in the new world of America. Judging by what you have seen so far, did they succeed? Explain.
4. What seems strange or demented about Roger Chillingworth?
5. Why do you think Hester is protecting the identity of the father of her child?
6. The Boston townspeople are labelling Hester as weak. Does she seem weak to you? Explain.
7. What does the Scarlet Letter symbolize? Explain.
8. Hester bears two symbols of her sin and shame. What are they? Explain.

THE SCARLET LETTER: PART II
TEACHER GUIDE

BACKGROUND

Hypocrisy is an inevitable part of any society, but its presence must be acknowledged and combated. Nathaniel Hawthorne felt this most keenly about the Puritan society he portrays in *The Scarlet Letter*, where the townspeople consider themselves to be morally righteous and cruelly judge the sins of others. Hawthorne was haunted by his family's Puritan past. In fact, his great-great-grandfather was John Hathorne, a judge who presided over the Salem Witch Trials. Hawthorne even added a *w* to his surname to further distance him from his Puritan ancestors.

Puritan society was devoted to creating "a city on a hill," an example of Christian living to which others could aspire. The Boston Hawthorne presents is a far cry from this ideal. Mercy and forgiveness, two fundamentals of Christianity, are missing from their actions. His point? Whenever people are unwilling to admit their own shortcomings, hypocrisy runs rampant, mercy dries up, and forgiveness becomes an impossibility.

In the Gospel of John a woman caught in adultery is brought before Jesus Christ by a crowd of angry townspeople, armed with stones. When asked what should be done with her, Jesus's answer derails their cries for her execution: "Let he who is without sin cast the first stone." The woman's accusers depart one by one. Then Jesus declares, "Neither do I condemn you. Go and sin no more." Mercy and forgiveness prevail. This story is a lesson that Hawthorne's Puritans seem to have forgotten.

SUMMARY

Hester, released from the jailhouse, takes up residence outside the town in a simple seaside cottage and earns her living by her needlework. The townspeople treat Hester cruelly, although they admire her seamstress skills

As her daughter, Pearl, grows up, Hester notices strange tendencies in her behavior. Pearl denies having a "heavenly Father" and claims to be born from a wild rosebush. She also seems to have a strange attraction to Hester's scarlet letter. Hester dresses Pearl in red, elaborately-stitched clothing.

Meanwhile, the young reverend Dimmesdale has fallen into poor health, and his congregation suggests that he share lodgings with Chillingworth, who has gained a reputation in the town as a doctor. Chillingworth suspects that the young reverend is hiding a dark secret and wants to discover it.

One day Hester visits the mansion of Governor Bellingham, where she encounters the town's two reverends and Chillingworth. Reverend Wilson greets Pearl but is disturbed by the way she answers questions about her faith. He tells Hester that there has been some talk of taking Pearl away from her. Hester becomes frantic, claiming that she is a fit teacher and parent for Pearl because of the lessons she has learned from the scarlet letter. Hester turns to Reverend Dimmesdale and begs him to intervene on her behalf, which he does. Chillingworth notes Dimmesdale's passionate plea for Hester and Pearl not to be separated. Reverend Wilson agrees that Pearl shall remain with Hester.

After this encounter, Mistress Hibbins, the governor's sister who has been suspected of witchcraft, invites Hester to one of the witch gatherings that happen in the forest. Hester replies that if the magistrates had taken Pearl away from her, she would have gladly joined them in their dark worship.

From the lodging they share, Dimmesdale and Chillingworth watch Hester and Pearl as they pass through the nearby graveyard. Chillingworth has guessed the source of Dimmesdale's illness, and when the young reverend is asleep, the doctor opens the front of Dimmesdale's shirt. The secret sight that Chillingworth sees on the young man's chest causes him to rejoice.

ESSENTIAL QUESTIONS

- Why is it important to forgive?
- Why is it important to own up when we have made a mistake?

CHARACTER ANALYSIS

Pearl Described as impish and wild, Pearl is Hester's scarlet letter brought to life. Pearl's odd behavior makes her seem supernatural at times: She can sense certain details about how she came to be born and feels a preternatural bond to her true father. At the beginning of the novel Pearl symbolizes sin and the effects of sin but later changes to a symbol of redemption.

ANTICIPATORY QUESTIONS

- What strategy do you think Chillingworth will use to find the father of Hester's child?
- Who do you think is the father of Hester's child?
- If you were Hester Prynne, would you move away to another town?

SYMBOLISM

- **Pearl's Name** Even though Pearl's birth is a source of dishonor for her, Hester chooses to name her "Pearl," a precious item—also a white (symbolically pure) item. This is also a reference to the "pearl of great price" mentioned in the parables of Jesus Christ (Matthew 13:45).
- **Pearl's Behavior and Clothing** As the little girl grows up, Pearl proves to be unruly and bizarre. This helps establish her as a personification of Hester's scarlet letter—the result of her own rule-breaking. On pg. 121 the author says that Hester could not discipline the child because of the way she had been created. On pg. 121 Hester dresses her daughter in red and elaborately decorates her as she has done to the scarlet letter. This strengthens the link between the letter and the girl who was created from the sinful act.
- **Reflection** On pg. 123 Hester sees her reflection, wherein the scarlet letter looms so large she cannot see her own face behind it. This is symbolic of the way Hester feels—trapped by her sin.

RECALL QUESTIONS

1. What does Hester do for a living?
2. What is strange about the way Hester dresses Pearl?
3. Who now lives with Reverend Dimmesdale, who is in poor health?
4. What have the leaders of the town discussed doing with Pearl?
5. Chillingworth cheers triumphantly after seeing something where?

THE SCARLET LETTER: PART II

CAST

HESTER	*Shunned Woman*
PEARL	*Daughter of Hester*
CHILD ONE	*Puritan Child*
CHILD TWO	*Puritan Child*
DAME	*Wealthy Woman*
POOR MAN	*Victim of Poverty*
GOVERNOR	*Colonial Magistrate*
WILSON	*Elderly Minister*
DIMMESDALE	*Young Minister*
CHILLINGWORTH	*Strange Physician*
M. HIBBINS	*Old Crone*
MAN ONE	*Church Member*
MAN TWO	*Church Member*

NARRATOR: Finally, Hester Prynne's term of confinement came to an end, and her prison door was thrown open. She came forth into the sunshine. Yet life for her had changed. She was now the symbol at which the preacher and moralist would point. She became the embodiment of woman's frailty and sinful passion. The young and pure were taught to look at her—and the scarlet letter flaming on her breast—as the figure and reality of sin. Clergymen paused in the street to lecture her, and if she dared to enter a church, to hear the Word of God beside her fellow townspeople, it was often her misfortune to become the topic of the sermon. Her sin was inescapable it seemed.

HESTER: *(to herself)* I can no longer borrow happiness from the future as others can—to help me through this present grief. What future do I have? Tomorrow will be just as today. And the next day and the next. Finally, when death comes to me, over my grave will hang the scarlet letter—my only monument.

NARRATOR: It may seem marvelous that this woman would continue to call Boston her home, where her shame was called to the attention of so many. But her sin and ignominy were the roots which she had stuck into the soil, and there she stayed planted.

HESTER: *(to herself)* Here is the scene of my guilt. Here shall be the scene of my earthly punishment.

NARRATOR: On the outskirts of the town, far from the dwellings of the other townspeople, stood a small, thatched cottage on the seashore. In this little, lonesome dwelling, Hester established herself and her infant child—using the slender means she possessed.

A mystic shadow of suspicion attached itself to the spot at once. Children would creep close to the cottage window and peek inside to spy Hester plying her needle.

CHILD ONE: *(whispering)* There is the woman—and her witch baby! They say that her scarlet letter is red-hot with the flames of hell! They say it glows when she walks around in the darkness!

CHILD TWO: Where *is* the letter? I don't see it!

CHILD ONE: (*in fright*) There it is! Run! Before it gets us with its hellfire!

(*sounds of children screaming and running*)

HESTER: Shhh, my little one. It is only children playing at games.

NARRATOR: To Hester's shock the first object that her infant daughter seemed to become aware of was the scarlet letter itself. Once the child reached up from the cradle, grasped at the letter, and would not let go. (*happy cry of a child*) But Hester tore the child's hand quickly away, gasping for breath.

HESTER: (*frightened*) No, my child! No.

NARRATOR: Although the scarlet letter was Hester's constant shame, she felt that it had also endowed her with a new sense. It gave her a sympathetic knowledge of the hidden sins in other hearts. Sometimes she would pass near a venerable minister or magistrate, and the red letter would give a throb.

HESTER: (*to herself, surprised*) Ah! What evil person is at hand? (*pause*) But there is no one here but this earthly saint.

NARRATOR: Or Hester would detect the eyes of a young maiden shyly glancing at the scarlet letter and then averting her eyes.

HESTER: (*to herself*) Behold, Hester. Here is a companion—a fellow sinner.

NARRATOR: It was by the art of her needlework that Hester supplied herself and her daughter with food. She had a delicate and imaginative skill with the needle, which she had displayed in the stitching of the scarlet letter. Her handiwork became the fashion in the colony. Her work was seen on the collar of the Governor, the scarves of the military men, the caps of well-to-do babies, and even in the coffins of the dead. But never was she called upon to embroider the white veil of a bride.

When she delivered her work, the dames for whom she sewed, frequently distilled drops of bitterness into Hester's heart.

HESTER: Here are the gloves I sewed for your late husband. I am sorry for your loss.

DAME: I do not need *your* pity. Be gone from here at once!

NARRATOR: Hester had schooled herself long and well and never responded to these attacks—except for a flush of crimson that rose over her pale cheek and then subsided into her bosom.

HESTER: Good day, mistress.

NARRATOR: Although she sewed magnificent garments for others, Hester's own dress was of the coarsest materials and most somber hue. Her only ornament was the scarlet letter. But her daughter's attire, on the other hand, was highly decorated.

Without a friend to be seen, through her craft, Hester was able to support herself. Any surplus money she made was given to the poor, who often scorned her for the kindness.

HESTER: Please. Take these garments that I have sewn for you. They are nothing much!

POOR MAN: I'll say! I don't need the charity of a worthless sinner.

HESTER: Please take them.

NARRATOR: In this way Hester came to have a part to perform in the world. Yet it was a world she no longer inhabited.

HESTER: Oh, my daughter. At least you are too young to know how they treat me. All that they do shows me I am banished from them. I am the inhabitant of another world. I am as a ghost that revisits a familiar fireside yet can no longer make itself seen or felt.

NARRATOR: Hester's only comfort was her daughter, Pearl. She gave her child that name because she was her only treasure—purchased with all that she had.

HESTER: You are my pearl of great price. It is strange. You are a consequence of my sin, and while I am punished by man for this sin, God has given you to me through it.

NARRATOR: As Pearl grew from an infant into childhood, Hester could not force herself to make her daughter abide by any rule or regulation. After all, a great law had been broken to create Pearl, so she was destined to be a child of disorder.

HESTER: *(frustrated)* Pearl, please behave! Please! Stand close by me!

PEARL: No, I will not! No!

NARRATOR: The child had such a wild flow of spirits and at times acted so strangely that Hester sometimes wondered whether Pearl was a human child—or not some sprite or fairy.

HESTER: Oh, Father in heaven—if you are still my Father—what is this being which I have brought into the world?

NARRATOR: Pearl would hear comments like this and smile knowingly at her mother with an unsettling grin.

Once as Pearl was flinging flowers at the scarlet letter upon her mother's bosom, Hester playfully asked…

HESTER: *(playfully)* Child, what are you?

PEARL: O, I am your little Pearl.

HESTER: Tell me truthfully—who are you and who sent you to me?

NARRATOR: Pearl stopped her game and sat earnestly near her mother's knees.

PEARL: You tell *me*, Mother. Tell me!

HESTER: Why…your heavenly Father sent you.

PEARL: I have no heavenly Father.

HESTER: Hush, Pearl! Hush! You must not talk so! He sent all of us into this world.

NARRATOR: But even Hester herself could not be sure that her child was not affected by an evil spirit. Many times, as a strange look came into Pearl's eyes, Hester thought she spied a fiend-like face in the black mirror of her eye. It was as if the evil spirit that possessed the child had just then peeped forth in mockery.

Hester adorned Pearl in the most ornate, delicate dresses of crimson hue. This, and the reputation of her mother, only made her more of an outcast from the other children. She was an imp—a product of sin—and she had no place among normal children.

CHILD ONE: Look! There is the woman of the scarlet letter!

CHILD TWO: And there is another scarlet letter walking by her side.

CHILD ONE: *(taunting)* Fairy-child! Fairy-child! Fly away! Fly away!

CHILD TWO: *(to Pearl)* My mother says you are the child of a demon!

CHILD ONE: Go back to your father! Go back, witch-baby!

CHILD TWO: Come on! Let's fling mud at them!

PEARL: *(shrieking)* Stop it! Leave me alone!

NARRATOR: In these instances, when provoked, Pearl would fly at the other children in a rage, slinging rocks toward them. They in turn would run away screaming in fright. *(frightened cries of children)*

PEARL: Flee! Or I will come for you! I will curse you with a spell!

HESTER: *(frightened)* Pearl!

NARRATOR: These outbursts frightened Hester, for Pearl's cries sounded like the curses of a witch.

HESTER: You should not treat the other children so.

PEARL: Why not? They deserve it. I wish I really could curse them with a spell.

HESTER: *(in shock)* Do not even say such things!

NARRATOR: Yet Hester could not punish the child because she knew Pearl's actions were merely the shadowy reflection of the evil that existed in herself.

Meanwhile, Hester's long-lost husband, who had returned, took up residence in the town under the name of Roger Chillingworth and presented himself as a physician. For the townspeople his sudden appearance surrounded him with an air of mystery.

About this time the health of young Reverend Dimmesdale began to fail. His form grew emaciated. His voice, though still rich and sweet, had a certain prophecy of decay in it. And he often placed his hand over his heart, followed by a pale face.

MAN ONE: Our goodly pastor studies too much, and it has caused his cheek to pale!

MAN TWO: Perhaps the doctor Chillingworth could aid him. They say he gathers herbs and digs up roots and knows all their mysterious properties.

MAN ONE: It is Providence that has placed the doctor here at just the right time. We must speak to Reverend Dimmesdale at once and urge him to accept this leech's services.

NARRATOR: The elders of the church and his fellow ministers approached Reverend Dimmesdale.

DIMMESDALE: I need no medicine.

WILSON: Heaven has sent you this aid, and it would be a sin to refuse it.

NARRATOR: So the reverend finally relented and agreed to accept the services of Roger Chillingworth.

DIMMESDALE: Doctor, I tell you the truth—when it is my time to pass from this earth, I am content.

CHILLINGWORTH: Ah, young men, not having taken a deep root, give up their hold on life so easily. And saintly men, who walk with God on earth, would happily be away to walk with him upon the golden pavements of the New Jerusalem.

NARRATOR: In this manner, the mysterious Chillingworth became the medical adviser of Reverend Dimmesdale. For the sake of the minister's health and to enable the doctor to gather his plants, they took long walks on the seashore. On many occasions one man was the guest in the home of the other, until, upon the suggestion of Chillingworth, it was finally arranged that the two should lodge together.

One day Hester Prynne journeyed to the mansion of Governor Bellingham to deliver a pair of gloves, which she had fringed and embroidered by his request for some official ceremony. This was one of her intentions. The other was to seek the truth concerning a rumor. Some had whispered that the Governor planned to remove Pearl from her care. Hester and Pearl approached the mansion, rapped the knocker, and were greeted by a servant.

HESTER: Is the worshipful Governor Bellingham within?

NARRATOR: The servant informed Hester that the governor was in the company of two ministers and a doctor and could not be disturbed.

HESTER: Nevertheless, I will come inside and wait. Come along, Pearl.

NARRATOR: The servant, thinking Hester must be some regal lady, let her inside the wide and lofty hall. The walls were lined with portraits that gazed out with harsh and intolerant criticism. Pearl looked up at them and wrinkled her nose.

PEARL: Look, Mother! There!

NARRATOR: A suit of armor stood further down the hallway, and Pearl ran ahead to admire the polished mirror of the breastplate.

PEARL: Mother, I see you in there! Look!

NARRATOR: The breastplate reflected Hester's image back—only incredibly distorted. The scarlet letter was represented in exaggerated and gigantic proportions so that it was the most prominent feature of her appearance and she seemed absolutely hidden behind it.

HESTER: Come along, Pearl. Come and look into this fair garden. It may be we shall find flowers there. Perhaps some more beautiful than the ones we find in the woods.

PEARL: I think that I shall have a rose!

HESTER: No, daughter. Those are not for you.

PEARL: I will have a rose.

HESTER: Hush, child! I told you, "No!"

NARRATOR: But Pearl would not be pacified, and she cried even louder.

PEARL: *(crying out)* I must have a rose! I must! I must!

HESTER: Hush! I hear voices approaching!

NARRATOR: Just then Governor Bellingham, Reverend Wilson, and Reverend Dimmesdale entered from the garden. The governor was surprised to see Pearl, adorned all in scarlet, standing seemingly all alone in the hall.

GOVERNOR: *(surprised)* What have we here? They say there used to be little spirits like these that appeared at holiday times. But, I wonder, how did this one become a guest in my hall?

NARRATOR: Hester started to move forward and announce her presence but drew back when she beheld the fourth man who accompanied the dignitaries: Roger Chillingworth. She was startled to perceive what a change had come over his features—how much uglier they were, how his dark complexion seemed to have grown duskier, and his figure more misshapen since the days when she had familiarly known him.

WILSON: *(playfully)* Yes, what little bird of scarlet plumage may this be? Pray tell me, young one, who are you? Why has your mother dressed you in this strange fashion?

NARRATOR: He gestured to Pearl's vibrantly red dress.

WILSON: Are you a Christian child? Do you know your catechism?

PEARL: *(indignantly)* I am my mother's child, and my name is Pearl.

WILSON: *(chuckling)* Pearl? Judging by your hue, you should instead be called "Ruby" or "Coral" or "Red Rose."

NARRATOR: The minister tried to kindly pat Pearl upon the head, but the girl shrank away from his touch.

WILSON: But where is this mother of yours? Ah! There I see her.

NARRATOR: At last they spied Hester in the shadows, and she nodded to them.

WILSON: Governor, this is the same child we were talking about. And behold here is the unhappy woman who is her mother.

GOVERNOR: She comes at a good time. We will look into this matter right away.

HESTER: What matter is that?

WILSON: Hester Prynne, the point has been weightily discussed, whether we who are in authority should trust the immortal soul of this child to the guidance of one who has stumbled and fallen amid the pitfalls of this world.

HESTER: You would take my child away from me?

NARRATOR: Hester pulled Pearl to her.

GOVERNOR: Surely you agree that it would be best for this little one's eternal welfare that she be taken out of your care. Other guardians could clad her soberly, discipline her strictly, and instruct her in the truths of heaven and earth. What can *you* do for her?

HESTER: *(passionately)* I can teach my little Pearl what I have learned from *this*!

NARRATOR: Hester pointed to the scarlet letter.

GOVERNOR: Woman, that is your badge of shame! It is because of the sinful stain that the letter indicates that we should transfer your child to other hands.

NARRATOR: Hester's features became suddenly calm.

HESTER: Nevertheless, this badge *has* taught me. It daily teaches me. It is teaching me at this moment. Its lessons can bring no profit to me, but they will make my child wiser and better.

WILSON: *(sigh)* Let me speak to the child. I am quite good with children.

NARRATOR: Reverend Wilson knelt, trying to coax Pearl to sit on his knee. Pearl stared at him strangely and clutched her mother's hand.

WILSON: Pearl, my child. I want to ask you a question. Can you tell me who made you?

PEARL: I was not made at all. My mother plucked me off the wild rose bush that grew at the prison door.

NARRATOR: Old Roger Chillingworth, with a smile on his face, whispered something in young Reverend Dimmesdale's ear.

GOVERNOR: *(in shock)* How awful! Here is a child of three years old, and she cannot tell who made her! Without question, she is equally in the dark as to her soul, her present depravity, and future destiny! I think, gentlemen, we need inquire no further!

NARRATOR: Hester grabbed Pearl up into her arms.

HESTER: God gave me this child! He gave her in place of everything else He has taken from me. She is my happiness—although she is my torture, as well. Don't you see? She *is* the scarlet letter! Only *she* can be loved. While I love her, she is also endowed with a millionfold retribution for my sin. You shall not take her! I will die first!

WILSON: *(kindly)* My poor woman, the child shall be well cared for—far better than you ever could.

NARRATOR: Hester turned suddenly to the young Reverend Dimmesdale, who looked up with his melancholy eyes.

HESTER: Speak for me! God gave her into my keeping. I will not give her up! You have sympathies that these men lack. You know what is in my heart. You know what a mother's rights are. You know how much stronger those rights are when that mother only has her child and the scarlet letter. Look to it! I will lose the child!

NARRATOR: Dimmesdale stepped forward with his hand over his heart.

DIMMESDALE: Gentlemen, is there not a quality of sacredness in the relation between this mother and this child?

GOVERNOR: What do you mean, good Master Dimmesdale? Make it plain, I pray you.

DIMMESDALE: This child comes from its father's guilt and its mother's shame. The child has come from the hand of God to work good upon her heart. The proof is how earnestly she pleads for the right to keep the child.

WILSON: The child is meant as a punishment for her sins as well.

DIMMESDALE: A torture to be felt! A pang, a sting, an ever-recurring agony in the midst of a troubled joy! Has she not expressed this thought in the garb of the poor child? It forcibly reminds us of that red symbol which sears her bosom!

WILSON: Well said again.

DIMMESDALE: This blessing was meant, above all things else, to keep the mother's soul alive—to preserve her from blacker depths of sin into which Satan might have sought to plunge her!

GOVERNOR: So you think that this situation is good?

DIMMESDALE: At every moment, her fall reminds her of the Creator's sacred pledge—if she brings the child to heaven, the child also will bring its parent there as well. In this way the sinful mother is happier than the sinful father. For Hester Prynne's sake, let us leave them as Heaven has seen fit to place them.

NARRATOR: Chillingworth, who had watched this interchange silently, moved forward—leering.

CHILLINGWORTH: You speak, my friend, with a strange earnestness.

WILSON: There is weighty importance in what my young brother has spoken. However, we must put the child to an examination in the catechism.

NARRATOR: As Reverend Wilson spoke further to the Governor, Pearl snuck close to Reverend Dimmesdale. She took his hand and caressed it gently against her cheek. He began to draw back his hand, but he saw Hester watching this intently.

HESTER: (*to herself*) Is that *my* Pearl?

NARRATOR: Dimmesdale looked over his shoulder and placed his other hand kindly upon Pearl's head. Then he hesitantly kissed her brow.

PEARL: (*giggling*)

NARRATOR: As Pearl danced away from the minister, he smiled. Chillingworth suddenly appeared at the minister's side.

CHILLINGWORTH: A strange child. It is easy to see the mother's part in her. What do you think, gentlemen? Would it be beyond a philosopher's skill to analyze the child's nature, and from its make and mold, make a shrewd guess at the father?

NARRATOR: Chillingworth glanced slyly at the young reverend.

WILSON: No. That would be sinful to use profane philosophy to answer such a question. It would be better to leave the mystery as we find it—unless Heaven reveals it of its own accord. Until then, every good Christian man has an obligation to show a father's kindness toward the poor, deserted babe.

NARRATOR: The men turned and made their exit. As Hester and Pearl began to leave, an old woman appeared out of the thick curtains of the hall, as if from nowhere. It was Mistress Hibbins, the sister to the governor.

MISTRESS HIBBINS: (*hissing*) Will you go with us tonight? There will be a merry company in the forest, and I would love to tell the Black Man that comely Hester Prynne should be with us.

HESTER: Had they taken Pearl from me, I would have willingly gone with you into the forest. I would have signed the Black Man's book, too—with my own blood!

NARRATOR: In the months following this encounter, Roger Chillingworth began to dig into his patient's heart like a miner searching for gold. He was searching for the confession of a secret that he sensed lay deep within the minister's soul. And as Reverend Dimmesdale's health continued to worsen, the townspeople whispered that the minister must be haunted by Satan himself—or Satan's emissary, in the guise of old Roger Chillingworth.

One day, as Dimmesdale leaned upon the window sill and stared into the nearby graveyard, the old doctor entered the lodging they now shared. In his hands he carried a bundle of unsightly weeds.

CHILLINGWORTH: I found these herbs growing on a grave which bore no tombstone—nor other memorial of the dead man—except these ugly weeds. I think that they may symbolize some hideous secret that was buried with him—a secret he should have confessed during his lifetime.

NARRATOR: Chillingworth watched the face of Dimmesdale shrewdly—searching for any kind of reaction to his comments.

DIMMESDALE: Maybe he earnestly desired to confess it—but could not.

CHILLINGWORTH: And why not? All the powers of nature call so earnestly for the confession of sin. These black weeds have sprung up out of a buried heart to make manifest an unspoken crime.

DIMMESDALE: There can be no power, short of Divine mercy, that can disclose the secrets that might be buried in a human heart. The heart must hold them—until the glorious day when all hidden things shall be revealed. But then not with reluctance but with joy unutterable at the last day.

CHILLINGWORTH: Then why not reveal those buried secrets here on earth? Why should not the guilty ones receive this blessed relief sooner?

DIMMESDALE: (*grim chuckle*) What a relief I have witnessed in these sinful brethren! Why should a wretched man, guilty of murder, prefer to keep the dead corpse buried in his own heart rather than fling it forth at once and let the universe take care of it?

CHILLINGWORTH: Yet some men bury their secrets like that.

DIMMESDALE: Guilty as they may be, they shrink from displaying themselves black and filthy in the view of men. Because, after that, no good can be achieved by them. No evil of the past can be redeemed by better service. So, to their own unutterable torment, they go about among their fellow creatures looking as new fallen snow, while their hearts are all speckled and spotted with iniquity of which they cannot rid themselves.

CHILLINGWORTH: These men deceive themselves then. They fear to take up the shame that rightfully belongs to them. If they seek to glorify God, let them not lift their unclean hands heavenward! O, wise and pious friend. Would you have me believe that a false show can be better than God's own truth?

NARRATOR: Before Dimmesdale could answer, they heard the clear, wild laughter of a young child's voice coming from the nearby graveyard. It was Pearl and Hester walking there.

PEARL: (*laughing*) Mother, hurry!

HESTER: Pearl! Please show reverence for the deceased!

NARRATOR: Ignoring her mother, Pearl skipped from one gravestone to another until she reached a large headstone—which she danced upon.

HESTER: Pearl, behave decorously!

NARRATOR: Pearl jumped from the gravestone and gathered up a handful of burrs from a nearby plant. Taking handfuls of these, she arranged them along the lines of the scarlet letter upon her mother's bosom.

HESTER: Pearl, please.

NARRATOR: But Hester did not pluck them off. Roger Chillingworth, who had watched Dimmesdale's reaction to all of this, smiled grimly.

CHILLINGWORTH: In this child there is no law—no reverence for authority. No concept of right or wrong. What, in Heaven's name, is she? Has she feelings? Has she any principles?

DIMMESDALE: None—only the freedom of a broken law. Whether she is capable of good, I do not know.

NARRATOR: Pearl, hearing voices, looked up with a naughty smile. Spying Dimmesdale in the window, she hurled a burr up at him. The clergyman shrunk back from the missile. Pearl clapped her hands wildly, and Hester looked up to behold the watchers in the window. All four of them regarded each other in silence—until Pearl laughed aloud.

PEARL: *(laughing)* Come away, Mother! Come away or that Black Man up there will catch you! He has got ahold of the minister already. Come away, Mother, or he will catch you! But he cannot catch little Pearl!

NARRATOR: So Pearl drew her mother away, skipping and dancing among the hills of the dead.

CHILLINGWORTH: There goes a woman, who has many flaws, but she has none of that hidden sinfulness, which you deem so grievous to be borne. Do you think Hester Prynne is less miserable for that scarlet letter on her breast?

DIMMESDALE: There was a look of pain in her face which I would gladly have been spared the sight of. But still, I think it is better for the sufferer to be free to show his pain, as this poor woman Hester is, than to cover it all up in his heart.

CHILLINGWORTH: A physical disease may even be the symptom of some ailment of the soul.

DIMMESDALE: Do you also deal in medicine for the soul?

CHILLINGWORTH: How may your physician heal the bodily evil—unless you first lay open to him the wound in your soul?

DIMMESDALE: No! Not to you! Not to an earthly physician! If it be the soul's disease, then I commit myself to the one and only Physician of the soul! He can cure—or He can kill. But who are you to meddle in this matter? Who dares to thrust himself between the sufferer and his God?

NARRATOR: With a frantic gesture Dimmesdale rushed from the room—with his hand shielding his heart. Chillingworth watched his departure calmly—with a grave smile.

CHILLINGWORTH: *(to himself)* It is well that I have made this step. We will be friends again soon. I now see pious Master Dimmesdale has done a wild thing before in the hot passion of his heart—and I will discover it.

NARRATOR: Later Chillingworth found Dimmesdale in a deep slumber, slumped in his chair with a large volume laid open before him. The physician walked forward and laid his hand upon the minister's chest, thrust aside the vestment that had always covered it, and stared in wonder.

CHILLINGWORTH: *(hissing)* Ah!

DIMMESDALE: *(muttering in his sleep)*

NARRATOR: Dimmesdale stirred but did not wake. Chillingworth turned with a wild look of ghastly rapture, threw his arms toward the ceiling, and stamped his feet upon the floor. It was the same way Satan rejoices when a precious human soul is lost to heaven and won into his kingdom.

DISCUSSION QUESTIONS

1. What is strange about Pearl? Why does she act in such a strange manner? How is she both a consolation and a curse to her mother?
2. Why does Pearl feel a special connection to the scarlet letter that her mother wears?
3. What is symbolic about the way Hester sees herself reflected in the suit of armor?
4. Is Reverend Dimmesdale right—once a person has been found guilty of sin, can he or she no longer do any good in the world? Explain.
5. What do you think Roger Chillingworth has discovered about Reverend Dimmesdale?

THE SCARLET LETTER: PART III
TEACHER GUIDE

BACKGROUND

Forgiveness and its power are a central theme of *The Scarlet Letter*. Hester, who has admitted her sin, receives forgiveness (to a degree) from her fellow townspeople. At least, they no longer see it as their duty to punish her for her sins. Reverend Dimmesdale craves forgiveness but cannot bring himself to openly admit his guilt. Yet it is Roger Chillingworth whose relationship with forgiveness is the most deadly. Since he is unwilling to give forgiveness to Dimmesdale and resolves himself to revenge, he becomes the vessel of unquenchable hatred. Unforgiveness has been compared to an acid. The container which harbors it suffers as much as the one it is used upon. Chillingworth transforms into an inhuman creature because of his unwillingness to forgive.

As with nearly all his fiction, Hawthorne attempted to teach a moral lesson, and *The Scarlet Letter* is his most effective lesson. While all of the main characters sin and suffer, it is Chillingworth who suffers the most, and his hatred proves to be his undoing.

SUMMARY

As the years progress, the Boston townspeople begin to view Hester's scarlet letter in a new light. They no longer see it as a badge of shame, but because of her pious actions, they now see it as a sign of honor. One sick man, to whom she attends, even comments that it must stand for "able." There is even talk that the letter has supernatural powers. According to rumor, it once stopped an Indian's arrow fired at Hester's bosom.

Meanwhile, Reverend Dimmesdale's condition worsens as he is continually tortured by Chillingworth. Ironically, as his guilt increases, his sermons become more and more effective. The minister dreams of confessing his sin, and in private he even whips himself to punish himself for his sin.

One night in a delusion Dimmesdale climbs the pillory in the town square. While he is standing there, Hester and Pearl pass by, and Dimmesdale calls out and asks them to join him. As they stand upon the scaffold all together, Pearl asks the minister if he will stand with them there tomorrow during the daylight, but Dimmesdale says they will never stand together until Judgment Day. Suddenly the red glow of a meteor lights up the night sky, and its trail forms a scarlet *A*. Chillingworth arrives at the scaffold and escorts the minister home. The next day the church sexton tells Dimmesdale one of his gloves was found upon the scaffolding but concludes that the Devil must have transported it there.

Hester longs to tell Dimmesdale that Chillingworth is actually her husband, so she goes to speak to Chillingworth as he gathers herbs along the seaside. She notices that Chillingworth looks more horrific and devil-like than before. She begs Chillingworth to forgive Dimmesdale for his own health, but he refuses. As Hester departs, Pearl shows her mother that she has made her own scarlet letter out of seaweed. Hester asks Pearl if she knows why she wears the scarlet letter. Pearl says it is the same reason the minister holds his hand over his heart. Hester leaves the beach vowing to make Chillingworth's identity known to Dimmesdale.

ESSENTIAL QUESTIONS

- Why is revenge harmful to the retaliator?
- What is destructive about secrecy and dishonesty?

CHARACTER ANALYSIS

Chillingworth As the novel progresses, Roger Chillingworth acts out his revenge with maniacal glee. Yet as his victim, Reverend Dimmesdale, deteriorates, Chillingworth does as well. This is reflected in his physical features as he becomes more devil-like and inhuman. Although Hester and Dimmesdale have both sinned, it is the sin of unforgiveness that is the greatest and ultimately claims Chillingworth. For this reason he is symbolic of unforgiveness.

ANTICIPATORY QUESTIONS

- What promise did Hester make to Roger Chillingworth?
- Have you ever seen a shooting star?
- Have you ever tried to cover up a lie? What was the result?

SYMBOLISM

- **The Scarlet Letter** While originally the scarlet *A* symbolized Hester's sin, the meaning of the letter changes as Hester continues to do good among her community. On pg. 133 one man even suggests that it stands for *able* instead of *adultery*.
- **Pillory** The town pillory is a place for criminals, and it symbolizes the shame of sin. For this reason Reverend Dimmesdale is drawn to it, and it is the spot where Dimmesdale, his love, and his child are reunited on pg. 135. It is only through sin that their family is formed. Although Dimmesdale is haunted by the pillory, it is eventually the place that will set him free from his sin.
- **The Meteor** On pg. 136 the light of the meteor in the sky illuminates Dimmesdale and his family upon the scaffolding. This can be symbolic of God's truth, while the darkness symbolizes lies and deceptions. This link is strengthened by the conversation Dimmesdale and Hester have concerning Judgment Day and the superstition among the townspeople that the meteor was a supernatural occurrence.
- **Chillingworth's Appearance** As the doctor continues his revenge against Dimmesdale, his physical appearance changes until Hester observes that he looks demon-like on pg. 139 and half-expects him to sprout bat wings and fly away on pg. 140. His outward appearance is a symbol of what has happened inwardly.

RECALL QUESTIONS

1. Where does Reverend Dimmesdale go to stand in the middle of the night?
2. What does Pearl ask Reverend Dimmesdale to do and he refuses?
3. What shape does the meteor in the sky form?
4. What item was found upon the scaffolding?
5. How has Chillingworth's appearance changed?

THE SCARLET LETTER: PART III

CAST

DIMMESDALE	*Guilt-stricken Minister*
CHILLINGWORTH	*Devious, Old Physician*
HESTER	*Fallen Woman*
PEARL	*Daughter of Hester*
SEXTON	*Church Official*
STRANGER	*Stranger to Boston*
WOMAN	*Citizen of Boston*
SICK MAN	*Dying Man*

NARRATOR: Over time an unexpected sense of regard grew up among the townspeople of Boston for Hester Prynne, one they had so violently shunned. With the scarlet letter and its fantastic embroidery on her breast, Hester had become a familiar object to the townspeople. When pestilence stalked through the town, no one was so devoted as Hester as she tended the sickbeds of many. In all seasons of calamity, the untouchables of society at once found her by their side. She came, not as a guest, but as a rightful inhabitant into any household that was darkened by trouble. It seemed gloomy twilight was the fitting time for her to hold intercourse with her fellow creatures. In the darkest of times there glimmered the embroidered letter—comfort coming from its unearthly ray.

SICK MAN: *(weakly)* I can never repay your kindness.

HESTER: There is nothing to repay.

NARRATOR: The letter was the symbol of her calling. Such helpfulness was found in her—so much power to do and power to sympathize with all types of calamity—that many people refused to interpret the scarlet letter by its original signification.

SICK MAN: *(weakly)* What a woman of strength. That letter...must stand for "able."

NARRATOR: So the townspeople began to look upon Hester and the scarlet letter differently.

WOMAN: Do you see that woman with the embroidered badge? She is our Hester—the town's own Hester—who is so kind to the poor, so helpful to the sick, so comforting to the afflicted!

STRANGER: What does that *A* signify—upon her bosom? Is it for some sin?

WOMAN: No, no. That is a symbol of the many good deeds she has done.

NARRATOR: The scarlet letter had the effect of the cross on a nun's bosom. It imparted to the wearer a kind of sacredness, which enabled her to walk securely amid all peril.

Had she fallen among thieves, it would have kept her safe. It was reported and believed by many that an Indian had fired his arrow against the badge, and when the missile struck, it fell harmlessly to the ground.

Also during this time, the stricken condition of young Reverend Dimmesdale worsened. A secret enemy was continually by his side—taking on the semblance of a friend and helper. Chillingworth the physician availed himself of every opportunity to tamper with the delicate springs of Reverend Dimmesdale's nature and drive him into an even weaker state.

Although he suffered in body and spirit, Reverend Dimmesdale achieved a brilliant popularity as a preacher. His words were filled with holy fire, and his congregation viewed him as the mouth-piece of Heaven. To them the very ground on which he trod was sanctified. His elderly church members even requested that their bones be buried close to their young pastor's holy grave.

Dimmesdale, too, thought of his grave and questioned whether the grass would ever grow upon it because of the accursed thing that would lie buried there. At times he longed to confess his sin.

DIMMESDALE: I, who have laid the hand of baptism upon your children—I, who have breathed the parting prayer over your dying friends—I, your pastor, whom you so reverence and trust...am utterly a pollution and a lie.

NARRATOR: Many times Reverend Dimmesdale had gone up into the pulpit, determined never to come down its steps until he had spoken his confession. But a true confession never came forth from his lips.

This inward struggle drove him to strange practices. In his secret closet, under lock and key, was a bloody scourge. Often he would take the scourge and strike it across his shoulders. Each lash and each stripe across his back was a physical punishment for his sin, which simultaneously hurt and relieved him. *(sound of a whip)*

DIMMESDALE: *(cries of pain and laughter)*

NARRATOR: He would also fast for days at a time, until hallucinations danced before him. He deprived himself of sleep and agonized over his iniquity.

One night as the young minister was haunted by guilty images of his sin, a sudden idea struck him, a way perhaps to unburden his soul. He hurried into the dark night.

DIMMESDALE: Yes! That was the scene of her guilt! Perhaps it will relieve me of mine!

NARRATOR: Dimmesdale reached the scaffold of the town pillory, where seven years before Hester had stood in front of her fellow townspeople in her shame. He climbed the steps and looked out over the darkened town. All was at rest.

As he stood there, Dimmesdale felt that the universe was staring at a scarlet token on his naked breast—right over his heart. On that spot there was (and had been for a long time) the gnawing and poisonous tooth of bodily pain. The reverend suddenly shrieked out—an outcry that went pealing through the night.

DIMMESDALE: *(cry of intense pain)* Ahhh! *(panting)* It is done! The whole town will awake, hurry forth, and find me here!

NARRATOR: But it was not so. The town did not awake. A light appeared in the governor's mansion—Mistress Hibbins, the governor's sister, peering out, thinking she had heard the sound of witches' cries. But it was soon put out.

Then a lantern appeared along the thoroughfare, and Dimmesdale recognized who carried it. It was Reverend Wilson, his fellow clergyman, coming home late from visiting a sickbed, for the elderly former governor Winthrop was passing away. The reverend passed beneath Dimmesdale, who was shrouded by darkness, without looking upward.

DIMMESDALE: (*strangely*) A good evening to you, Reverend Wilson. Come up here and pass a pleasant hour with me.

NARRATOR: Dimmesdale started in shock. Had he actually spoken these words? But Reverend Wilson passed on, and Dimmesdale realized the words had only been uttered in his imagination.

DIMMESDALE: I will only have to stand here until morning. Soon the entire town will awake and find me, their minister, Arthur Dimmesdale, upon the scaffold—bathed in the red light of dawn. Imagine their shock! (*laughs*)

NARRATOR: His laugh was answered by another—a light, childish laugh. (*laugh of a child*)

DIMMESDALE: That laugh! Pearl! Little Pearl! Hester! Hester Prynne! Are you there?

NARRATOR: Dimmesdale could make out two forms passing by the scaffolding below.

HESTER: Yes, it is I—and my little Pearl. I have been watching at Governor Winthrop's deathbed and have taken a measurement for a robe.

DIMMESDALE: Come up here, Hester, you and little Pearl. You have both been up here before, but I was not with you then. Come up here once again, and we will stand all three together!

NARRATOR: Hester silently ascended the steps and stood upon the platform, holding little Pearl by the hand. The minister felt for the child's other hand and took it. The moment that he did so, there came what seemed a rush of new life pouring like a torrent into his heart and hurrying through all his veins. It was as if the mother and child were communicating their vital warmth to his system. The three formed an electric chain.

DIMMESDALE: (*sighing*) Ah!

NARRATOR: But the minister's relief was soon interrupted.

PEARL: Minister, will you stand here with Mother and me tomorrow at noontide?

NARRATOR: The dread of public exposure, that had so long been the anguish of his life, returned upon Dimmesdale.

DIMMESDALE: No. I cannot, little Pearl. I shall stand with you and your mother someday—but not tomorrow.

NARRATOR: Pearl began to pull her hand away.

DIMMESDALE: Stay a moment longer, my child!

PEARL: But will you promise to take my hand and Mother's hand tomorrow at noontide?

DIMMESDALE: Not then, Pearl, but another time.

PEARL: What other time?

DIMMESDALE: At the great Judgment Day. Then and there before the judgment seat, your mother, you, and I must stand together. But the daylight of this world shall not see our meeting.

NARRATOR: Before Dimmesdale had finished speaking, a light gleamed far and wide over the muffled sky.

DIMMESDALE: *(in shock)* Look!

NARRATOR: It was undoubtedly caused by a meteor, and its powerful radiance filled the street with all the light of midday. They stood in the noon of that strange and solemn splendor—the minister, with his hand over his heart, Hester with the embroidered letter glittering on her bosom, and little Pearl, herself a symbol—the connecting link between the two. It was as if it were the celestial light that will one day reveal all secrets, and the daybreak that shall unite all who belong to one another.

Perhaps it was because of his mental disease or a true supernatural phenomenon, but as the minister glanced up at the sky, he beheld an immense letter *A* marked out in lines of dull, red light. Then the light faded, and they were left in darkness once again.

DIMMESDALE: Do my eyes deceive me?

PEARL: Look, minister.

NARRATOR: Pearl pointed down to the base of the scaffold.

DIMMESDALE: *(gasp)*

NARRATOR: There stood Roger Chillingworth, and for a moment the mask of kindness he continually wore had been dropped. He was staring up at Dimmesdale with a diabolical look of hatred, and the minister was overcome with terror.

DIMMESDALE: Who is that man, Hester? I shiver at him! Do you know the man? I hate him, Hester.

NARRATOR: Hester remained silent. She remembered the oath she had made to Chillingworth.

PEARL: Minister, I can tell you who he is!

DIMMESDALE: Quickly then, child! Quickly! And tell me as low as you can whisper.

NARRATOR: Dimmesdale bent down to the child's lips, but Pearl mumbled gibberish into his ear—as children are apt to do. Then she looked at him with an elf-child grin.

PEARL: *(laugh)*

DIMMESDALE: Do you mock me now?

PEARL: You are not bold! You are not true! You would not promise to take my hand and Mother's hand tomorrow at noontide!

NARRATOR: Chillingworth called up through the darkness.

CHILLINGWORTH: Worthy sir. Master Dimmesdale, can this be you? I must keep a closer eye on you. You must have walked here in your sleep. Come, my dear friend, let me lead you home.

DIMMESDALE: *(fearfully)* How did you know I was here?

CHILLINGWORTH: Truthfully, I knew nothing of the matter. I spent the better part of the night at the bedside of a dying man, using my poor skill to give him ease. He is going home to a better world. I likewise was on *my* way home when this strange light shone out. Come with me. Otherwise, you will not be able to do Sabbath duty tomorrow.

DIMMESDALE: I will go home with you.

NARRATOR: With a chilly despondency, like one awakening from an ugly dream, Dimmesdale yielded himself to the doctor to be led away. Hester watched them depart together.

HESTER: He is at the threshold of lunacy—if he has not crossed over it. Is it out of fear that I keep my oath to his torturer? Or is it because I'm trying to save him from a blacker fate? I must find a way to help him if I can. He deserves that much.

NARRATOR: The next day Dimmesdale preached the richest and most powerful sermon he had ever preached. But as he came down the pulpit steps, the church sexton met him, holding a black glove, which the minister recognized as his own.

SEXTON: This was found this morning on the scaffolding.

NARRATOR: Dimmesdale nearly swooned. For a time he had begun to think the previous night had been only a dream or vision.

SEXTON: Satan must have dropped it in that shameful place to play a joke on a holy man like you.

DIMMESDALE: Thank you, my good friend. Yes, it seems to be my glove indeed.

SEXTON: And did you hear of a portent last night—a great red letter *A* in the sky? We interpreted it to mean "Angel" because Former-Governor Winthrop was made an angel this past night.

DIMMESDALE: No. I had not heard of it.

NARRATOR: As time passed on, Hester did not forget the plight of Dimmesdale and at last resolved to meet with Chillingworth, her former husband, and do what might be in her power to rescue his victim. The occasion was not long to seek. One afternoon, while walking with Pearl, Hester beheld the old physician with a basket in one arm and a staff in the other hand, stooping along the ground in quest of roots and herbs to concoct his foul medicine. His gray beard almost touched the ground as he crept about.

HESTER: Pearl, run along the beach while I speak with this man.

CHILLINGWORTH: Ah, Mistress Hester. Do you have a word for old Roger Chillingworth? I hear good tidings of you these days! I heard one of the magistrates discussing your case. He said it has been suggested that the scarlet letter be taken off your bosom. On my life, I encouraged him to do so!

HESTER: They cannot take off this badge. If I were worthy to be rid of it, it would fall away all on its own—or be transformed into something that speaks a different meaning.

CHILLINGWORTH: Wear it then—if it suits you better. A woman must follow her own fancy concerning how she adorns herself.

NARRATOR: It had been long since Hester had seen Chillingworth, and she was shocked to see how he had changed. The studious, calm, and quiet intellectual she had married was no longer there. He now had a fierce look about him, a look that he fought to keep hidden behind a smile. But from time to time his true nature would break forth in a spasm and reveal his blackness all the more.

Chillingworth was striking evidence that a man has the power to turn himself into a devil if he will only, for a time, take on the devil's office. This unhappy man had undergone this transformation by devoting himself to the torture of a guilty heart.

As Hester observed all this, the scarlet letter throbbed on her chest.

HESTER: *(to herself)* Here is another life ruined—by my hand.

CHILLINGWORTH: What do you see in my face that you look at so earnestly?

HESTER: Something that would make me weep—if there were any tears bitter enough for it. But let it pass! It is of another miserable man that I would speak.

CHILLINGWORTH: *(eagerly)* Ah! I know of whom you speak! What of him? My thoughts were just now busy with that gentleman.

HESTER: Some years ago you forced a promise of secrecy from me—concerning the former relation between yourself and me. Since the life and good name of that man were in your hands, there seemed no choice for me. Yet it was with heavy misgivings that I bound myself to this promise. Although I had thrown off all duty to other human beings, I felt I had a duty to him—and I betrayed it by pledging myself to you.

NARRATOR: Chillingworth smiled as she said this.

CHILLINGWORTH: Yes. I remember it well.

HESTER: Since that day, no man has been nearer to him as you. You tread behind his every footstep. You are beside him, sleeping and waking. You search his thoughts. You burrow and tinker in his heart! Daily you cause him to go through a living death. Still he does not know you for what you really are. In permitting this, I have been false to the only man to whom I have the power to be true.

CHILLINGWORTH: What choice had you? My finger, pointed at this man, would have hurled him from his pulpit into the dungeon—and then to the gallows.

HESTER: It would have been better so!

CHILLINGWORTH: What evil have I done the man? I tell you, Hester, kings could not afford the care that I have given this wretched priest! If not for *my* aid, his life would have burned away in torments within the first two years after the perpetration of his crime—your crime together. His spirit lacks the strength of yours—to bear up under the burden of the scarlet letter. He breathes and creeps about on the earth, and it is all owing to me!

HESTER: Better he had died at once!

NARRATOR: A glare of red light came from Chillingworth's eyes, as if the old man's soul were on fire.

CHILLINGWORTH: *(chuckling)* Yes, woman, you speak truth. Never has a mortal suffered what this man has suffered. And all in the sight of his worst enemy! He senses my true nature, but he has not pinpointed it. He has felt an influence working on him always like a curse. He imagines that he has been given over to a fiend—to be tortured with frightful and desperate dreams—as a foretaste of what awaits him beyond the grave. He did not err! There is a demon at his elbow! A mortal man, with a once-human heart, has become a devil especially for his torment!

HESTER: Have you not tortured him enough? Has he not paid you enough?

NARRATOR: For a second Chillingworth allowed all the evil within him to be written upon his features.

CHILLINGWORTH: (*devilishly*) No! No! He has only increased the debt! Do you remember me as I was nine years ago? I was once a kind, thoughtful man. Was I not?

HESTER: All this—and more.

CHILLINGWORTH: And what am I now? I have already told you what I am—a fiend! Who made me so?

HESTER: (*passionately*) It was myself! It was I, more than he. Why not avenge yourself on me?

CHILLINGWORTH: I have left you to the scarlet letter. If it has not avenged me, I can do no more.

NARRATOR: He laid his long finger on the scarlet letter with a smile.

HESTER: It has avenged you.

CHILLINGWORTH: I thought as much. Now, what do you want to speak with me concerning this man?

HESTER: I must reveal your true character to him. I do not know what result this will have. But what good is it for him to live such a life of ghastly emptiness? Do with him what you will! Announce him! Send him to the gallows! There is no good for him, no good for me, no good for you, no good for little Pearl. There is no path to guide us out of this dismal maze.

NARRATOR: Suddenly, there was a look of admiration on Roger Chillingworth's face.

CHILLINGWORTH: Woman, I pity you. If you had met with a better love than mine, this evil might have been avoided. I pity you for the good in you that has been wasted.

HESTER: And I pity you. Hatred has transformed you from a wise and just man into a demon. Will you purge it out of you and be human once more? If not for his sake, then for your own! Forgive him! Leave this further retribution to the Power that rightfully claims it! We are all wandering in this dark maze of evil—stumbling over our own guilt. But there might be good for you. You are the only one with the power of pardon. Will you reject that priceless benefit?

CHILLINGWORTH: Peace, Hester, peace. It is not in my ability to pardon. I have not the power you speak of. My old faith, long forgotten, comes back to me. It explains all we do—all we suffer. From your first step astray, you did plant the seed of evil. But since that moment, all this has been a dark necessity. You that have wronged me are not sinful—except in a kind of illusion. Neither am I demon-like. It is our fate. Let the black flower blossom as it may. Now go your way and deal as you will with that man.

NARRATOR: So the deformed, old figure, whose face haunted men's memories longer than they liked, took leave of Hester Prynne and went stooping away along the earth, continuing to gather herbs and roots.

Hester gazed after him a little while, with a curiosity to see whether the tender spring grass would be blighted beneath his footsteps. Perhaps he would suddenly sink into the earth, leaving a barren and blasted spot behind. Perhaps he would spread bat's wings and flee away, looking uglier the higher he rose toward heaven.

HESTER: Be it a sin or not—I hate the man. He has done me worse wrong than I did him! *(pause)* Pearl! Where is my little Pearl?

PEARL: Here I am, Mother!

NARRATOR: Pearl had gathered seaweed and made herself a scarf, mantle, and headdress—decorating herself to look like a little mermaid. As the last touch she took some eel-grass and made on her bosom a letter *A*—but freshly green instead of scarlet.

PEARL: Mother! See my letter *A*? Are you going to ask me what it means?

NARRATOR: Hester smiled mirthlessly.

HESTER: The green letter on you has no meaning. But do you know what this letter *I* am doomed to wear means?

PEARL: Of course, Mother. It is the great letter *A* that you taught me in the schoolbook.

NARRATOR: Hester stared into Pearl's little face. Did she really attach some meaning to the letter?

HESTER: Do you know, my child, why I wear this letter?

PEARL: Yes. It is the same reason the minister holds his hand over his heart.

HESTER: What has the letter to do with any heart except mine?

PEARL: I do not know, Mother. I have told you all that *I* know. Perhaps you should ask that old man you were speaking to. Perhaps he can tell you. *(pause)* But tell me, Mother, truly—what does the letter mean? And why does the minister hold his hand over his heart?

NARRATOR: Pearl took her mother's hand in her own and gazed into her eyes with an earnestness that was seldom seen in her wild and capricious character. For the first time, Hester considered telling Pearl the truth. Perhaps she was old enough to share her mother's burden. Perhaps heaven had sent Pearl to her, not as a curse, but as a merciful blessing—a fellow soul to share her troubles.

HESTER: *(to herself)* No! If that is the price I must pay for a child's sympathy, I will not pay it. *(aloud)* Silly Pearl! What questions are these? There are many things in this world a child must not ask. I wear the scarlet letter for the sake of its golden thread.

NARRATOR: But the child did not see fit to let the matter drop. She asked as her mother and she went homeward at suppertime, while Hester was putting her to bed, and after she seemed to be asleep. Each time Pearl looked up with mischief gleaming in her black eyes.

PEARL: Mother, what does the scarlet letter mean? Why does the minister keep his hand over his heart?

HESTER: *(angrily)* Hold your tongue, naughty child! Do not tease me! Or I will put you into the dark closet!

NARRATOR: But Hester's anger was mainly turned against herself. She felt remorse that she had made a bargain that placed Dimmesdale, one she had once loved, in so much torment.

HESTER: This must end. I must make Roger Chillingworth's true nature known to the victim of his tortures. Then let come what may.

DISCUSSION QUESTIONS

1. How does the symbolism of the scarlet letter change in this portion of the story?
2. Although Dimmesdale is under extreme psychological torture, his sermons become more effective. Why is this so?
3. Since Dimmesdale feels he cannot confess, what other techniques does he use in a vain effort to rid himself of his guilt?
4. Why is Hester's public shame much less terrible than Dimmesdale's private shame?
5. What is the meaning of the meteor and the red *A* drawn in the sky?
6. Why will Pearl not be kind to Reverend Dimmesdale?
7. Why is Chillingworth's sin more despicable than Hester and Dimmesdale's?
8. What will Dimmesdale do once he finds out Chillingworth's true identity?

THE SCARLET LETTER: PART IV
TEACHER GUIDE

BACKGROUND

Symbolism pervades *The Scarlet Letter*. In fact, literary critics hail the novel as the first symbolic novel written in America as well as the first sign that the American novel could rival the best work of the Europeans. Needless to say, nobody does symbolism like Nathaniel Hawthorne. One of the most interesting facets of Hawthorne's symbols is their ambiguity. Nothing is ever as it seems. At the conclusion of the novel when Reverend Dimmesdale publicly confesses, there is still confusion as to what actually happened. Some townspeople claim to have seen a letter scratched upon his chest, although they attribute it to different causes, while others maintain there was nothing there at all. Still others claim the minister never even confessed in the first place. Hawthorne, the only person who could clear up this confusion, leaves the truth of the matter up to the reader.

Similarly, the symbols within the story are in a constant state of flux. The scarlet letter symbolizes different things at different points in the story. Even settings like the forest symbolize different things to different people. So what is Hawthorne's intention in all this ambiguity?

One of the many themes of the book is the warning to reserve judgment against the sins of others. Those of us who may seem pure on the outside have deep, dark secrets, and those of us who seem to be polluted past all hope still have the chance of redemption. Hawthorne urges us not to cast judgment, to hope for the best, and forgive the flaws of others as we remember our own. His symbols remind us of that message.

SUMMARY

Hester has decided to make Chillingworth's true identity known to Reverend Dimmesdale, but she can never find a time to tell the minister this news in secret, so she travels into the forest in hopes of intercepting him there. Hester encounters Dimmesdale in the forest as he returns from visiting a missionary to the natives. The two speak of their misery, and Dimmesdale tells Hester that she is fortunate to wear her sin openly for all to see, for he is tortured by his own guilt in secret. Hester tells Dimmesdale that Chillingworth is her husband and has been secretly torturing him. Dimmesdale says that somehow he has always known this to be true but also says he cannot forgive Hester for hiding this from him. Hester demands his forgiveness, and Dimmesdale relents. Hester tells Dimmesdale that they should leave Boston together and start a new life elsewhere. Hester removes the scarlet letter from her dress and lets her hair down from her cap. When Pearl sees Hester, she is wary to approach her mother—refusing to until Hester puts the letter back on her dress. Hester does so and conceals her hair once again. After this is done, Pearl returns to her mother. Hester and Dimmesdale make a plan to leave on a ship for Europe, and Dimmesdale says that he must first preach the Election Sermon. They return to town with this plan in place.

The day of the Election Sermon arrives, and the captain of the ship that Hester has commissioned tells her that Chillingworth has also booked passage aboard it. Dimmesdale preaches his sermon, but as he passes the pillory scaffolding, he nearly faints. He then climbs the scaffold and confesses his sin. He tears open his shirt to reveal (according to some witnesses) an *A* scratched into his own chest. His confession complete, he falls down and passes away with Hester and Pearl beside him. Pearl kisses her father before he dies.

Soon after this Chillingworth passes away and leaves all his wealth to Pearl. Hester takes Pearl to Europe, where she becomes a regal lady. Years later Hester returns to Boston and lives out the rest of her days there. When she dies, she is buried next to Dimmesdale, and on her tombstone is a scarlet *A*.

ESSENTIAL QUESTIONS

- Is there such a thing as redemption?
- Even though we make mistakes, can we still do good works in the world?

CHARACTER ANALYSIS

Dimmesdale No character in the novel is more tragic in than the guilt-ridden minister, Reverend Dimmesdale. Crippled by his inability to face his own flaws and admit his guilt, Dimmesdale robs himself of a life of happiness with his true family. Dimmesdale represents the effects of guilt.

ANTICIPATORY QUESTIONS

- Do you think Dimmesdale will ever confess his sin?
- How do you think the townspeople would react if Dimmesdale confessed?
- If Dimmesdale accepted Pearl as his daughter, how do you think that would change him and her?

SYMBOLISM

- **The Forest** Throughout the story, the forest is referenced as the domain of the Devil, and for most of the townspeople it symbolizes evil. Yet it is the forest where Dimmesdale and Hester first had their romance, and it is the only place they are now allowed to be together. In this sense it also symbolizes freedom and solace.
- **Forest Sunshine** On pg. 145 Pearl plays in the forest sunshine, but when she invites Hester to touch a ray of sunlight, the ray vanishes. This is symbolic of Hester's suppression and unhappiness.
- **Hester's Hair** On pg. 149 when Hester removes her cap and allows her hair to fall free, it is as if Hester removes the burdens her society has placed upon her. After she does this, sunshine beams into the forest. When her beauty is confined once again, the forest seems to grow dimmer, and the shadow of gloom returns.

RECALL QUESTIONS

1. Where does Hester meet with Reverend Dimmesdale?
2. Why is Pearl frightened of her mother?
3. What plan do Hester and Dimmesdale make to find freedom?
4. Before the gathered townspeople, what does Dimmesdale reveal upon his body?
5. What appears on Hester's tombstone?

THE SCARLET LETTER: PART IV

CAST

HESTER	*Fallen Woman*
PEARL	*Daughter of Hester*
DIMMESDALE	*Young Minister*
CHILLINGWORTH	*Old Physician*
CAPTAIN	*Captain of a Ship*
M. HIBBINS	*Old Crone*

NARRATOR: Hester Prynne had resolved to make Roger Chillingworth's true identity known to Reverend Dimmesdale. Yet she did not know how to find the minister alone. She feared to go to his private study, for Chillingworth was always at his side. Then she heard that Dimmesdale had journeyed into the wilderness to visit a missionary to the Indians. So Hester journeyed into the woods, with Pearl trailing along, in hopes of intercepting the minister. As they traveled, the gray clouds above were stirred by a breeze, which caused gleaming flickers of sunshine to play along the path.

PEARL: Mother, the sunshine does not love you! It runs away and hides because it is afraid of something on your bosom. Now see! There it is over there! I will run and catch it! I am just a child, and it will not flee from me! I wear nothing on my bosom yet.

HESTER: Nor will you ever, I hope.

PEARL: Why not, Mother? When will my letter come to me? Will my letter come of its own accord when I am a grown woman?

HESTER: Run away, child, and catch the sunshine. It will be gone soon.

NARRATOR: Hester smiled as Pearl danced in a patch of sunshine. Hester drew nigh enough to step into the magic circle of light.

HESTER: See? Now I can stretch out my hand and grasp some sunshine, too.

PEARL: It will go now!

NARRATOR: Before Hester could touch the light, it disappeared. It was as if Pearl had absorbed the light into herself. Hester lowered her hand.

HESTER: Come along, my child. We will sit down a little way further into the woods and rest ourselves.

PEARL: I am not weary, Mother. But you may sit down. Will you tell me a story?

HESTER: A story? About what?

PEARL: Oh, a story about the Black Man! How he haunts this forest and carries a big, heavy book with iron clasps. He offers everybody who meets him the chance to write their name with their blood in his book.

HESTER: And who told you this story, Pearl?

PEARL: The old dame in the chimney-corner at the house where you watched last night. But she fancied me asleep while she was talking of it. She said that a thousand people had met the Black Man in the forest here—and ugly, old Mistress Hibbins was one of them. And, you, too, Mother. She said the scarlet letter was the Black Man's mark on you. She said it glows like a red flame when you meet him at midnight here in the dark wood. Is it true, Mother? And do you go to meet him in the nighttime?

HESTER: Did you ever wake up at night and find your mother gone?

PEARL: Not that I remember. If you fear to leave me alone in our cottage when you go to meet him, you may take me along with you. I would very gladly go! But tell me now—is there really a Black Man? And did you ever meet him? And is that his mark?

HESTER: Will you be at peace once I tell you?

PEARL: Yes, if you tell me.

HESTER: Once in my life I met the Black Man! This scarlet letter *is* his mark.

NARRATOR: They had seated themselves in a little dell with a brook flowing through the midst, over a bed of fallen and drowned leaves.

PEARL: O brook! O foolish and tiresome brook! Why are you so sad? What does this sad little brook say, Mother?

HESTER: If you had a sorrow of your own, the brook might tell you of it—even as it is telling me of mine. But now, Pearl, I hear footsteps along the path. Go play and leave me to speak with the one who comes yonder.

PEARL: Yes, Mother, but if it is the Black Man, may I stay a moment and look at him with his big book under his arm?

HESTER: Go, silly child! It is no Black Man! It is the minister!

PEARL: And look! He has his hand over his heart! Is it because, when the minister wrote his name in the book, the Black Man set his mark in that place? But why does he not wear it outside his bosom as you do, Mother?

HESTER: Go now, child! But keep close enough to hear the babble of the brook.

NARRATOR: So Pearl left her mother behind and set herself to the task of gathering flowers. Hester Prynne made a step or two toward the forest path, but still remained under the deep shadow of the trees. She beheld the minister advancing along the path entirely alone, leaning on a staff. He looked haggard and feeble. His hand was over his heart.

HESTER: Arthur Dimmesdale!

NARRATOR: Under the trees Dimmesdale observed a dark form that he did not know as woman or shadow. Then he saw the scarlet letter.

DIMMESDALE: Who speaks? Hester! Hester Prynne! Is it you? Are you in life?

HESTER: Yes, if my life can be called that. And you, Arthur Dimmesdale, do you still live?

NARRATOR: And so they met like two spirits reunited beyond the grave. Arthur Dimmesdale put forth his hand, chilly as death, and touched the cold hand of Hester Prynne—reassuring himself that they were inhabitants of the same world. They sat down beneath the trees and spoke like a pair of casual acquaintances—and finally turned to deeper subjects.

DIMMESDALE: Hester, have you found peace?

NARRATOR: She looked down to the scarlet letter.

HESTER: Have you?

DIMMESDALE: None! Nothing but despair. What else could I expect—being what I am and leading such a life as mine? If I were an atheist—a man without a conscience—I would have found peace long ago. Hester, I am most miserable!

HESTER: The people highly esteem you and surely you are working good among them. Does this not bring you comfort?

DIMMESDALE: Only more misery. What can a ruined soul like mine do for the redemption of other souls? And as for the people's reverence—I wish it was turned to scorn and hatred!

HESTER: You wrong yourself in this. In truth, your life is no less holy than it seems in people's eyes. Your life is filled with good works. Can they not bring you peace?

DIMMESDALE: You are happy because you wear the scarlet letter openly upon your bosom. Mine burns in secret! You do not know what a relief it is, after the torment of seven years, to look into eyes that recognize me for what I am! If I had one friend—or even a bitter enemy—who could see me as the vilest of sinners, my soul could keep itself alive. Even that much truth would save me! But now all is falsehood! All is emptiness! All is death!

HESTER: You wish for such a friend to weep with you, but you have one in me, your partner in sin. *(pause)* And you also have an enemy like you spoke of. You dwell with him—under the same roof.

DIMMESDALE: *(gasp)* What say you?

NARRATOR: The minister started to his feet, gasping for breath, and clutching at his heart, as if he would have torn it out of his chest.

HESTER: O Arthur! Forgive me! In everything else I have striven to be true. Truth was the one virtue which I might have held fast to! And I *did* hold fast—until your life and your fame were put into question. Then I consented to a deception. But a lie is never good—even though death threatens on the other side. Do you not see what I have to say? That old man, the physician whom they call Roger Chillingworth—he was my husband!

NARRATOR: Dimmesdale sank down on the ground and buried his face in his hands.

DIMMESDALE: I did know it—somehow. At the first sight of him I felt it in the natural recoil of my heart—and every time I have seen him since. Why didn't I understand? Oh, Hester Prynne, you know little about the horror of this all! The exposure of a sick and guilty heart to the very eye that would gloat over it! Woman, woman, I cannot forgive you!

NARRATOR: Hester flung herself on the fallen leaves beside the man she still passionately loved.

HESTER: You shall forgive me! Let God punish! You shall forgive!

NARRATOR: She threw her arms around him and pressed his head against her bosom, little caring though his cheek rested on the scarlet letter.

HESTER: Please! Do not frown upon me! All the world has frowned on me—for seven long years. I bore all their scorn and did not die. But I could not bear yours and live.

DIMMESDALE: I do forgive you, Hester! May God forgive us both! *(pause)* We are not the worst sinners in the world. There is one worse! Although I am a polluted priest, that old man's revenge has been blacker than my sin. He has violated, in cold blood, the sanctity of the human heart. You and I, Hester—we never did so.

HESTER: Never, never! What we did had a consecration of its own. We felt it so! We said so to one another. Have you forgotten it?

DIMMESDALE: I have not forgotten.

NARRATOR: As they reminisced, lingering there longer and longer under the trees, they tried not to think of the path that led back to the settlement, where Hester must take up again the burden of her shame and the minister the hollow mockery of his good name.

DIMMESDALE: How am I to live while breathing the same air with this deadly enemy? Think for me, Hester! You are strong. Resolve this for me!

HESTER: You must no longer dwell with this man. Your heart must no longer be under his evil eye.

DIMMESDALE: It is far worse than death! But how can I avoid it? What choice remains to me? Shall I lie down here and die at once? The judgment of God is upon me! I am not strong enough to struggle against it.

HESTER: Heaven would give you mercy—if you had the strength to grasp it.

DIMMESDALE: You must be strong for me.

HESTER: Then I must ask—is the world so narrow? Does the universe only lie within the compass of yonder town? Where does this forest path lead? Back to the settlement, you might say. Yes, but onward, too! And deeper it goes—deeper into the wilderness. A few miles from here the yellow leaves show no sign of the white man's tread. There you are free! Is there not enough shade in this boundless forest to hide your heart from the gaze of Roger Chillingworth?

DIMMESDALE: Yes, Hester. But only under the fallen leaves.

HESTER: Then there is the broad pathway of the sea! It brought you here. If you so choose, it will bear you back again. In our native land, whether in some rural village or in vast London, you would be beyond his power and knowledge!

DIMMESDALE: I am powerless to go. Wretched and sinful as I am, I have had no other thought than to drag on my earthly existence in the sphere where Providence has placed me.

HESTER: You will leave the weight of your misery behind you. There is good to be done. Exchange this false life of yours for a true one. Let your spirit summon you to such a mission to be the teacher and apostle of the red men. Or, if it would better fit your nature, be a scholar and a sage among the wisest and most renowned of the cultivated world. Preach! Write! Act! Do anything—except lie down and die! Give up this name of Arthur Dimmesdale and make yourself another—one you can wear without fear or shame. Up and away!

DIMMESDALE: O Hester! You talk of running a race to a man whose knees are tottering beneath him. I must die here! There is not the strength or courage left in me to venture into the wide world alone!

HESTER: You shall not go alone!

NARRATOR: A hope came into Dimmesdale's eyes, and he rose from the ground.

DIMMESDALE: Do I feel joy again? Hester, you are my better angel! I flung myself—sick, sin-strained, and sorrow-blackened—down upon these forest leaves but have risen up made anew. God has been merciful! This is already the better life! Why did we not find it sooner?

HESTER: Let us not look back. The past is gone. Why should we linger upon it now? See! With this symbol, I undo it all and make it as if it had never been.

NARRATOR: Hester undid the clasp that fastened the scarlet letter and, taking it from her bosom, threw it upon the bed of the stream, where it glittered like a lost jewel.

HESTER: Oh! Exquisite relief!

NARRATOR: By another impulse she took off the formal cap that confined her hair, and down it fell upon her shoulders, dark and rich. All at once, the sunshine burst forth and poured into the dreary forest—a sudden smile of heaven.

HESTER: You must know Pearl—our little Pearl. You have seen her before, I know, but you will see her with new eyes. She is a strange child. I hardly comprehend her. But you will love her dearly as I do. You will advise me how to deal with her.

DIMMESDALE: I am not good with children. I have even been afraid of little Pearl! Do you think she will be glad to know me?

HESTER: She will love you dearly! She is not far off. *(calling out)* Pearl! Pearl!

NARRATOR: Pearl, her hair and neck decorated with wild flowers, heard her mother's call but approached slowly when she saw the minister standing there.

HESTER: See with what natural skill she has made those simple flowers adorn her? Had she gathered jewels in the wood, they could not have become her better. Do you not think she is beautiful? I know whose brow she has! Yours, Arthur.

DIMMESDALE: Many times I have noticed that some of my own features are revealed in her face. I feared that the world might see them there. But she is mostly yours.

HESTER: Do not let her see anything strange—no passion nor eagerness—in your way of accosting her. Our Pearl does not tolerate emotion when she does not fully comprehend the reason behind it. But she loves me, and she will love you, too!

DIMMESDALE: No child can stand me. Even babies cry out when I hold them. Yet Pearl took my hand at the governor's mansion. You cannot understand how my heart dreads this interview—and yearns for it at the same time!

NARRATOR: By this time Pearl had reached the margin of the brook and stood on the further side, gazing silently at Hester and the clergyman, who unconsciously brought his hand to his chest.

DIMMESDALE: I have the strange feeling that this brook is the boundary between two worlds. She seems an elfish spirit from childhood legends that is forbidden to cross a running stream. Please tell her to come across.

HESTER: Come, Pearl! How slow you are! Here is a friend of mine, and he must be your friend also. You will have twice as much love given to you from now on. Leap across the brook and come to us.

NARRATOR: But Pearl remained on the other side of the brook.

HESTER: Hurry, Pearl, or I shall be angry with you!

NARRATOR: Pearl whined, stomped her feet, and gestured wildly at her mother's breast.

HESTER: I see what ails the child. Children will not abide the slightest change. Pearl misses something, which she has always seen me wear every day of her life. Pearl, there it is before you! On the side of the brook. Bring it here!

NARRATOR: There lay the scarlet letter so close upon the margin of the stream that the gold embroidery was reflected in it.

PEARL: *You* come and take it up!

HESTER: (*sigh*) She is right. I must bear the torture of the hateful token a little longer—until we shall leave this region and go to the land we have dreamed of. I cannot leave it here. The forest cannot hide it! One day, the ocean will take it from my hand and swallow it forever.

NARRATOR: Hester stepped to the bank, took up the scarlet letter, and fastened it again onto her bosom. A sense of doom returned upon her as she received back this deadly symbol. She had drawn an hour's free breath. And now the scarlet misery was glittering on the same, old spot. She next gathered up the heavy tresses of her hair and confined them beneath her cap. It was as if there were a withering spell in the sad letter. Her beauty, the warmth and richness of her womanhood, departed like fading sunshine, and a gray shadow seemed to fall across her.

HESTER: Do you know your mother now, child—now that she has her shame upon her once again—now that she looks sad again?

PEARL: Yes, I do now. Now you are my mother indeed! And I am your little Pearl.

NARRATOR: In a mood of tenderness that was not usual with her, Pearl crossed the brook, drew down her mother's head, and kissed her brow and both her cheeks. Then Pearl kissed the scarlet letter, too.

PEARL: Why does the minister sit over there?

HESTER: He waits to welcome you. Come and entreat his blessing! He loves you, and he loves your mother, too.

PEARL: *Does* he love us? Will he go back with us—hand and hand—into the town?

HESTER: Not now, dear. But in days to come he will walk hand in hand with us. We three will have a home and a fireside of our own. And you will sit upon his knee. He will love you. Will you love him back?

PEARL: Will he always keep his hand over his heart?

HESTER: Foolish child, what kind of question is that? Come and ask his blessing.

NARRATOR: But it was only through force that Hester was able to drag Pearl close to Dimmesdale. The clergyman, hoping that a kiss might ease the child's antipathy toward him, impressed one upon her brow.

PEARL: *(shrieking)* No!

NARRATOR: Pearl broke away from her mother and, running to the brook, washed the unwelcome kiss from her forehead. She then remained apart, silently watching Hester and the clergyman while they talked together and made arrangements for the future. They resolved that in order to be free they must return to the Old World.

HESTER: There is a ship in the harbor that will depart in four days' time. In my dealings with the townspeople I have made acquaintance with the captain. I can secure us passage for two individuals and a child.

DIMMESDALE: In three days' time the new governor will be instated, and I am to preach the Election Sermon. It will be a fitting end to my career here. Never let it be said that I did not fulfill my duty!

NARRATOR: With this plan in place, Hester and Dimmesdale parted company. Dimmesdale hurried townward at a rapid pace—new energy and life flowing through him. When he reached the town, he passed old Mistress Hibbins, the reputed witch-lady. Perhaps the old witch read the minister's thoughts, but she came to a full stop and looked shrewdly into his face.

MISTRESS HIBBINS: So, reverend, have you been visiting the forest? The next time please give me a fair warning, and I shall be proud to accompany you. I will put in a good word for you with my master.

DIMMESDALE: What do you mean? I was in the forest—visiting a missionary to the red men.

MISTRESS HIBBINS: *(cackling)* Oh, you carry it off very well! You must speak so here during the daytime. But at midnight we will talk more freely.

NARRATOR: This interview unnerved the minister, and he returned quickly to his home, closing himself in his study. Soon after there was a knock at the door, and Roger Chillingworth himself entered. All of the minister's old horror washed over him at the sight of this man. Dimmesdale stood white and speechless—clutching his Bible and his heart.

CHILLINGWORTH: Reverend, you look pale. Your journey through the forest has wearied you. Please partake of some of my medicine. You must be well to deliver your Election Sermon.

NARRATOR: Dimmesdale struggled to compose himself and smile at his tormentor.

DIMMESDALE: Oh no. The air has done me good. I think I will need no more of your drugs, my kind physician.

CHILLINGWORTH: Then you are cured—at long last! I joy to hear it!

DIMMESDALE: I thank you from my heart, my most watchful friend.

NARRATOR: Chillingworth grinned as he departed. The minister sat, breathing deeply, and, contemplating the joy of his future, began work upon his Election Sermon.

The day of the Election Sermon arrived, and many strange faces showed themselves in Boston. The city streets were thronged with spectators. Hester Prynne and little Pearl came into the marketplace. Wherever they went in the crowd, a vacant circle appeared around them. It was the effect of the scarlet letter.

HESTER: *(to herself)* Look your last on the scarlet letter and its wearer! Yet a little while, and she will be beyond your reach!

PEARL: Mother, why have all the people left their work today? Is it a playday for the whole world? And there are strangers here, too! Sailors! Why have they come to the marketplace?

HESTER: They're here to see the procession pass for the new governor.

PEARL: Will the minister be here? Will he hold out his hands to me—like he did beside the brook?

HESTER: He will be here, but he will not greet you today. And you must not greet him either.

PEARL: What a strange, sad man is he! In the darkness he calls to us and holds our hands. And in the forest, where only trees can hear, he talks to you and kisses me. But here, in the daylight, among all these people, he does not know us.

NARRATOR: As Hester and Pearl observed the festivities, a man with a feathered hat and a sword approached them. He was the captain of the *Spanish Main*, the ship on which Hester had secured passage.

CAPTAIN: Madam, everything has been arranged! I have made room for one more individual on our voyage.

HESTER: One more? What do you mean? Do you have another passenger?

CAPTAIN: Why yes! The physician here has decided to share passage with you. You must have known it! He tells me he is of your party and a close friend of the gentleman you spoke of.

NARRATOR: Even with her soul in turmoil, Hester's face remained calm. The captain tipped his hat and disappeared into the crowd. At that instant Hester beheld old Roger Chillingworth himself, standing in the corner of the marketplace and smiling a smile at her with a secret meaning.

HESTER: *(to herself)* All of our plans will be thwarted.

NARRATOR: Before Hester could call together her thoughts, the sound of music was heard. *(music)* It announced the arrival of the procession of magistrates and citizens on its way toward the meeting-house. Among the procession Hester spied Dimmesdale. There was no feebleness in his step, his frame was not bent, and his hand did not rest upon his heart.

PEARL: Mother, is that the same minister that kissed me by the brook?

HESTER: *(whispering)* Hold your peace, dear little Pearl! We must not talk in the marketplace of what happens to us in the forest.

NARRATOR: Behind Hester appeared Mistress Hibbins, richly decked in her finest gown for the occasion.

MISTRESS HIBBINS: Can you tell, Hester? Is that the same man you encountered on the forest path?

HESTER: Madam, I do not know what you speak of.

MISTRESS HIBBINS: Fie! Fie! I have been to the forest many times. Don't you know I have the skill to judge who else has been there? I see the Black Man's token on you. But Reverend Dimmesdale hides his mark from the eyes of all the world. *(cackling)*

PEARL: What is it, good Mistress Hibbins? Have you seen it?

MISTRESS HIBBINS: My darling, you will see it, one time or another. They say, child, you are the daughter of the Prince of the Air! Will you ride with me some fine night to see your father? He will tell you why the minister keeps his hand over his heart! I promise you that! *(cackling)*

NARRATOR: Laughing so shrilly that all the marketplace could hear her, the weird old gentlewoman took her departure. By this time the procession had reached the meeting-house, and the voice of Reverend Dimmesdale could be heard commencing his sermon. Hester and Pearl moved through the crowd to the foot of the nearby scaffold and stood there statue-like.

At last Dimmesdale finished his discourse. It had been the greatest sermon of his career. Those who heard it would not have been surprised if he had ascended into heaven upon its completion. But instead, as he finished, he looked suddenly weak once again.

Dimmesdale climbed down and, stumbling somewhat, joined the recession of dignitaries. As he passed the scaffold, he tottered forward. Borne up by supporting arms, Dimmesdale staggered toward where Hester and Pearl stood. His face seemed hardly the face of a man alive, with such a death-like hue. Yet he shook off the aid of the other men and stepped forward. He stared at Hester and Pearl with a tender and triumphant look on his face.

DIMMESDALE: *(weakly)* It is time. Hester, come here. Come, my little Pearl.

NARRATOR: Pearl, with a bird-like motion, flew to him and clasped her arms about his knees. The magistrates stared at this in puzzlement. Suddenly and violently, Roger Chillingworth thrust himself between them and caught the minister, his victim, by the arm.

CHILLINGWORTH: Madman! What is your purpose? Wave back that woman! Cast off this child! All shall be well! Do not blacken your fame! Do not perish in dishonor! *I can save you!* Would you bring infamy upon your sacred profession?

DIMMESDALE: Ha! You tempter! You are too late! Your power is not what it once was! With God's help, I shall escape you now.

NARRATOR: He extended his hand to Hester.

DIMMESDALE: Hester Prynne, in the name of Him so terrible and merciful who gives me grace, come here now and twine your strength around me! Support me to yonder scaffold!

NARRATOR: Hester moved to support Dimmesdale with her shoulder, and together they began to ascend the scaffold steps with Pearl between them. Roger Chillingworth followed behind, a fellow actor in the drama of guilt and sorrow who must be present at its closing scene.

Watching from below, the crowd could not understand what they saw and stared in awed silence.

CHILLINGWORTH: *(rasping)* No! In the whole earth there is no place that you could have escaped me—except on this very scaffold!

DIMMESDALE: Thanks be to Him who has led me here!

NARRATOR: Reaching the top platform of the scaffold, Dimmesdale turned to Hester with a feeble smile upon his lips.

DIMMESDALE: Is it not better than what we dreamed of in the forest?

HESTER: Better? We both may die and little Pearl with us.

DIMMESDALE: God is merciful! Let me now do the will which He has made plain before my sight, for I am a dying man. Let me take my shame upon me!

NARRATOR: Dimmesdale turned to address the crowd below.

DIMMESDALE: People of New England! You that have deemed me holy! Behold me here, the one sinner of the world! At last, I stand upon the spot where, seven years ago, I should have stood—here with this woman, whose arm sustains me at this dreadful moment. See the scarlet letter that Hester wears? You have all shuddered at it! Yet there stood another in the midst of you, who hid his own brand of sin and infamy upon him. God's eye beheld it! The Devil knew it well and seared it with the touch of his burning finger! Now, at the death hour, this man stands up before you! He bids you look again at Hester's scarlet letter! He tells you that it is but the shadow of what he bears on his own breast! Does anyone here question God's judgment on a sinner? Behold! Behold the dreadful witness of it!

NARRATOR: Dimmesdale ripped open his shirt. The crowd gasped at what they beheld there. *(crowd gasping)* With a look of triumph fixed on his face, Dimmesdale fell in a heap upon the scaffold. Hester knelt and tenderly supported his head. Chillingworth knelt down, too—defeated.

CHILLINGWORTH: You have escaped me! You have escaped me!

DIMMESDALE: *(weakly)* May God forgive you. You, too, have deeply sinned.

NARRATOR: Dimmesdale withdrew his dying eyes from the old man and fixed them on the woman and the child.

DIMMESDALE: *(to Pearl)* My little Pearl. Will you kiss me now? You would not in the forest. Will you now?

NARRATOR: Pearl kissed her father. It was as if a spell had been broken, and tears flowed from her eyes onto his cheek. Those tears were the pledge that she would do no more battle with the world but be a woman in it.

DIMMESDALE: Hester. Farewell.

HESTER: Shall we not meet again? Shall we not spend our immortal life together? Surely—surely we have ransomed one another with all this woe. Look into eternity with those bright, dying eyes. Tell me what you see.

DIMMESDALE: Hush, Hester. When we forgot God's law, I fear it became vain to hope that we should meet hereafter in an everlasting and pure reunion. But God knows, and He is merciful! He has proved his mercy in my afflictions. He gave me this burning torture upon my breast. He sent yonder dark and terrible man to keep the torture red-hot. He brought me to die a death of triumphant shame before the people. Had any of these agonies been wanting, I would have been lost forever! Praised be His name! His will be done! Farewell!

NARRATOR: That final word came forth with the minister's expiring breath. The multitude, silent until then, broke out in a strange, deep voice of awe and wonder. *(cry of shock and wonder)*

Long after the fact, there were many accounts of what was seen and heard that day. Most of the spectators testified that they saw a scarlet letter imprinted on the flesh of the minister's chest. Some speculated that the minister had carved the letter there as a penance. Others said it had appeared there through the necromancy of Roger Chillingworth. Still others said it was God's judgment—the body's outward expression of what was hidden in the minister's soul. Some said they saw nothing at all there.

And while some watchers swore they heard the reverend confess to being the father of Pearl, others said that this had not been so. Others justified his confession by saying that the kindly reverend, knowing that he was at the point of death, had only claimed so to share in Hester Prynne's shame.

As for Roger Chillingworth, all his strength and energy seemed to desert him at once, so that he positively withered up, shriveled away, and almost vanished from mortal sight, like an uprooted weed that lies wilting in the sun. When there is no more devil's work to do, the demon returns to his master. At his decease, which took place within the year, his last will and testament bequeathed a very considerable amount of property to little Pearl. So Pearl, the elf-child, the demon-offspring, became the richest heiress of her day in the New World. This circumstance wrought a great change in the public estimation of her. Had she stayed in the New World until a marriageable age, she would have found many an eager husband. But, not long afterward, Hester and Pearl disappeared—perhaps boarding a ship for the Old World. Rumors of them came back from over the sea.

After years had passed and the events associated with the scarlet letter had become the stuff of legend, Hester Prynne returned to Boston one day without explanation and took up residence again in the same simple cottage by the sea. The scarlet letter was still upon her breast, but Pearl was no longer with her. If she was still alive, she would have been in the bloom of young womanhood. It was rumored that Pearl had married a lord in the Old World and started a family of her own. Such a daughter would have happily had her mother there with her, but there was more life for Hester here in New England. Here had been her sin, her sorrow, and here was yet to be her penitence. She had returned and taken up the badge of shame of her own free will.

Never afterwards did it quit her bosom. As she lived out her days, doing good to all, the scarlet letter ceased to be a stigma, attracting the world's scorn and bitterness, and instead became something to be sorrowed over and looked upon with awe and reverence, too.

At last when Hester passed away, she was buried in the churchyard next to the grave of Reverend Dimmesdale but far enough away to suggest that the dust of the two sleepers had no right to mingle, even in death. There was a single tombstone raised over them. Upon its sable surface was one ever-glowing point of light, gloomier than the shadow—the scarlet letter *A*.

DISCUSSION QUESTIONS

1. In many old stories the wilderness symbolizes evil. It is where the Devil walks and witches meet. In *The Scarlet Letter* is the forest a setting for good or evil? Or both? Explain.
2. Why does the image of Hester without the scarlet letter frighten Pearl?
3. Dimmesdale does not know of Chillingworth's plan to follow him and Hester to Europe. Why does he decide to confess?
4. What do you think was actually on Dimmesdale's chest?
5. Is it fair that Dimmesdale, Hester, and Pearl are denied the chance to live together as a family? Explain.
6. Why does Chillingworth simply shrivel up and wither away after the death of Dimmesdale?
7. Why does Hester decide to return to Boston?
8. Does Pearl have a happy ending?
9. What has Hester Prynne's life proved about sin, shame, and forgiveness? Explain.
10. Think back to the beginning of the story when the narrator described a wild rosebush growing by the rusted-over prison door. What could the rosebush symbolize? Explain.

NEW WORLD COLONY-BUILDING GAME

Welcome to the New World! You have led a hearty band of settlers from the old world of Europe to establish a new home in the wilds of North America. As the governor of your colony, you will have to provide for the safety, health, and happiness of your colonists. Winter is fast approaching and to ensure that your colonists survive, you must strategically build up your colony!

Object of the Game: Build the colony with the most colonists and provide them with enough grain and social stability to survive through the winter.

Gameplay: Buying different types of buildings for your colony increases the number of colonists, the number of bushels of grain your colony harvests, and the colonists' happiness level. (Note: You can only build a maximum of *three* of each type of building.) As you build each building, subtract the building's cost from the treasury funds and write the building down on your colony map. When all the treasury funds have been spent, you cannot build any more buildings, winter comes, and gameplay is over. It is time to calculate your final score. During the winter each colonist eats a bushel of grain. Any colonist who does not have a bushel of grain to eat during the winter dies. The overall happiness level of the colonists determines if your number of colonists will increase or decrease during the winter months as well. The player who has the highest number of surviving colonists wins!

Calculating Your Score: When your treasury funds equal zero, winter comes. This means that the game is over, and it is time to calculate your score.

1. Each colonist eats one bushel of grain over the course of the winter. Subtract your number of colonists from your bushels of grain. If the result is a negative number, remove this many from your number of colonists. (You did not have enough grain to feed them all.)
2. Depending on their happiness level, your colonists will either dwindle or thrive during the winter months. **Note:** You do *not* have to provide grain for these bonus colonists! Add in the effects of your Happiness score:

Happiness Level	Effect
Less than 6	− 50 from your final number of colonists
6-10	+ 0 to your final number of colonists
11-15	+ 25 to your final number of colonists
16-20	+ 50 to your final number of colonists
Over 20	+ 75 to your final number of colonists

3. Whichever player has the highest number of colonists wins!

MAP OF YOUR COLONY COLONY NAME: _____

Number of Colonists	Treasury Funds ($)	Bushels of Grain	Happiness Level
10	400	0	0

_____ + _____ = _____
Surviving Colonists   **Happiness Level Effect**   **Final Score**

LIST OF COLONY BUILDINGS: You can only build 3 of each building type. If you build a building multiple times, you receive its effect multiple times as well.

BUILDING TYPE	EFFECT
Apothecary Shop: The apothecary attends to your colonists' medical needs. Happiness increases. **Cost:** $ 15	+ 2 to happiness
Barracks: Your colony can host a garrison of soldiers, and safety increases dramatically. **Cost:** $ 25	+ 20 to number of colonists
Blacksmith: Your colonists increase their productivity through the use of quality metal tools. **Cost:** $ 25	+ $ 35 to treasury funds + 5 to bushels of grain
Church: Your colonists can worship and gather together freely. **Cost:** $ 15	+ 10 to number of colonists + 1 to happiness
College: More people move to your colony for their education at your newly-built divinity school. **Cost:** $ 25	+ 15 to number of colonists
Factory: Colonists can manufacture items to sell to other colonies. **Cost:** $ 25	+ $ 35 to treasury funds + 15 to number of colonists
Field: You increase the amount of land that your colonists can farm. **Cost:** $ 35	+ 20 bushels of grain
Governor's Mansion: You build yourself a nice mansion. This attracts more rich colonists, but the poor colonists begin to grumble against you. **Cost:** $ 25	+ 13 to number of colonists - 2 from happiness

Harbor: Your seaside colony can trade better with other colonies. **Cost:** $ 25	+ 10 to number of colonists + 15 to bushels of grain
Marketplace: Your colonists can trade goods more freely. **Cost:** $ 25	+ $ 50 to treasury funds + 15 to bushels of grain
Meetinghouse: Your colonists can meet to discuss ideas and events. Their happiness increases. **Cost:** $ 15	+ 2 to happiness
Mill: Your colonists can grind their grain and use it more efficiently. **Cost:** $ 35	+ 20 to bushels of grain
Pillory: The crimes of the people are punished publicly, and safety increases. **Cost:** $ 10	+ 1 to happiness
Quarters: You build housing so that your colonists do not have to build their own homes. **Cost:** $ 35	+ 20 to number of colonists
Printing Press: Your colonists become more educated by freedom of the press. **Cost:** $ 15	+ 1 to happiness
Trading Post: Your colonists can trade with local Native American tribes. **Cost:** $ 25	+ $ 45 to treasury funds + 15 to bushels of grain
Warehouse: Your colonists can better store and preserve their grain. **Cost:** $ 25	+ 20 to bushels of grain

ABOUT THE AUTHOR

Zachary Hamby is a teacher of English in rural Missouri, where he has taught English for many years. He realizes the immediate need for students to understand, appreciate, and embrace the American Dream through American Literature and history. For this reason he has created the *Searching for America* textbook series that focuses specifically on connecting modern students to classic American Literature. His other book series is *Reaching Olympus*, consisting of materials designed for teachers of mythology. He is also a professional illustrator and a proud American. He resides in the Ozarks with his wife, Rachel (also an English teacher), and their two children.

For more information and products (including textbooks, posters, and electronic content) visit his website: **www.creativeenglishteacher.com**

Contact him by email at **hambypublishing@gmail.com**

www.ingramcontent.com/pod-product-compliance
Lightning Source LLC
Chambersburg PA
CBHW080736230426
43665CB00020B/2760